THE ART OF CALENDAR DESIGN

GINGKO PRESS

THE ART OF CALENDAR DESIGN

ISBN 978-1-58423-583-5

First Published in the United States of America by
Gingko Press by arrangement with
Sandu Publishing Co., Ltd.

Text edited by Gingko Press.

Gingko Press, Inc.
1321 Fifth Street
Berkeley, CA 94710 USA
Tel: (510) 898 1195
Fax: (510) 898 1196
Email:books@gingkopress.com
www.gingkopress.com

Copyright © 2015 by Sandu Publishing
First published in 2015 by Sandu Publishing

Sponsored by Design 360°
– Concept and Design Magazine

Edited and produced by
Sandu Publishing Co., Ltd.

Book design, concepts & art direction by
Sandu Publishing Co., Ltd.
Chief Editor: Wang Shaoqiang

info@sandupublishing.com
www.sandupublishing.com

All rights reserved. No part of this publication may
be reproduced or transmitted in any form or by any
means, electronic or mechanical, including photocopy,
recording or any information storage and retrieval
system, without prior permission in writing from the
publisher.

Printed and bound in China

CONTENTS

006	Preface
009	Chrono - Shredder
010	Date (Igenic Calendar)
012	Cycle Binaire
014	3D Calendar & Dish Dryer Rack, Wooden Engraving
016	See Nothing Calendar
018	2013 Wood Block Calendar
020	Bit Planner
022	Christmas Calendar
024	Reveal the Day
026	Calendar Design
028	Transformable Calendar
030	Calendar "Carpe Diem!"
032	Watching Calendar
034	Trash Calendar
036	Light Year 2015 Calendar
038	Planet Calendar
040	Calendar
042	1m.Tear off Calendar
044	The Tea Calendar
046	Weather
048	The Cube Calendar
050	Monthly Measure
052	Skyscraper Calendar
054	30x12 Exposé
058	MoMA Perpetual Calendar
060	Land Rover Topographic Calendar
062	YCN Competition Fedrigoni Desktop Calendar 2015
064	'70s Rock Calendar
066	Calendar Transformer Kit 2014
070	2015 Fedrigoni Calendar
072	Corian Calendar
074	Year'Round Perpetual Calendars
075	Game Calendar 2014
078	The 2012 Lovers' calendar
080	Calendar
081	Ice Sandwich Calendar
082	Chocoaday
084	Ring Calendar

086	Fedrigoni 2015 Desk Calendar	164	YCN Student Competition 2014 / Fedrigoni Calendar 2015 "LANDSCAPE"
088	Right Person, Wrong Time		
090	Fedrigoni Perprtual Desk Calendar: "22 Colours, 132 Weights,166 Days"	166	Time is a Gift
		168	Planet Calendar / 2013
092	Fedrigoni Woodstock 2015	172	Tea Life
094	Taylor Made Time	174	Botanical Life
096	Everlasting Adhesive Calendar	176	365 – Memory Calendar
098	Zivaaane Filtertips Calendar	178	Numerario (venti numeri 365 giorni)
100	Haglöfs Interactive Calendar	180	Calendar: Strictly Type
104	Calendar Design	182	2014 Calendar
106	2014 Typeface Calendar for Holiday	184	Calendar About the Sea
108	Fragile Pocket Calendar	186	Periodic Table of Time
110	Bar Calendar	188	"Pull Up Yourself to Face New Challenges" Calendar
112	Twelve Horses 2014		
114	Art Catalog for Severija Inčirauskaitė – Kriaunevičienė	189	Two Thousand Ten
		190	Calendar "Graphic Design"
116	Calendar	192	Planetary Calendar 2014
118	Time Zone Calendar	194	Calendar Concordia Design
120	YCN Fedrigoni Calendar	196	Multiply Calendar
122	Calendar Design of 2014	198	Conceptual Series of Poster - Calendar "4392"
124	NEWWORK Calendar 2014	200	Studio Lin x Linco 2014 Calendar
126	Calendar-Pop-up Poem Book	202	Embroidery Calendar
130	Invisible Calendar	204	Dia Calendar
132	Student Organizer - Time is of the Essence	206	Mühleisen and Partner Calendar
134	2012 Lo Siento Calendar	208	SNGP CALENDAR
136	Natural (2014 Calendar)	210	Saisonkalender 2014 für Obst & Gemüse
138	Studio Lin x Linco 2012 Calendar	212	Calendar for the Firefighters
140	Bearded Calendar	214	*Life is a Presto* Music Note Calendar
142	FPCEUP Calendars	215	Typographic Calendar
144	Pocket Planner 2013	216	Calendar<Motion>
146	YCN Fedrigoni Competition Brief 2014	218	Night Calendar
148	Gong Xi Fa Cai	220	Black Calendar
150	2015 Fedrigoni Calendar	222	The Simple Calendar
152	Calendar Planetarium	224	Die-cut Wall Calendar
154	Vasava Calendar	226	Calendar 2014
156	Ando Calendar – 'The Twelve of '13'	228	FAB 365 Calendar
158	CIMIYIK Color Matching Calendar	230	United Bamboo 2011 Cat Calendar
160	2015 Fedrigoni Paper Desk Calendar	232	Haircuts Calendar
162	Dragon Year Calendar	233	Index
163	Bird & Tree	240	Acknowledgements

PREFACE

The Calendar is Dead. Long Live the Calendar.

Let's be honest, why would anyone use a wall or desktop calendar these days? I never used one until I designed one myself. That makes me wonder if maybe everyone should just design their own calendar when they really need it. For instance, my father creates a calendar every year as a family Christmas gift. Its print run is approximately 12. Apart from a simple but clear overview of the days and months of the year, it features photographs of our family members, one or two per month. This is an extremely exclusive calendar. It's not available for sale, and can only be found in the houses of our relatives. The images are emotionally appealing and the length of the month determines their lifespan, making each family member visible for about 30 days.

People used to hang calendars on their wall as a form of decoration; perhaps they still do, although I seem to see it less and less. The images they featured seemed to express a longing for the past, and inspired feelings of nostalgia. The best-known paintings of a famous artist, historical cityscapes, or cute animals hung on display for a month at a time. As a child, I was always eager to leaf through them, excited to find out what image was waiting to be revealed on the first day of the new month.

My grandparents had a birthday calendar on their wall, a cheerful calendar with dates on it on which they wrote down people's birthday. A perpetual calendar with an unambiguous goal: to remind them of the important moments in their life.

All of which brings me back to my original question: why would I want to use, let alone design, a physical calendar?

I have always been fascinated by systems and their underlying structures; I find great enjoyment in gazing at intricate, well-made, and brilliantly conceived objects, like a motor or a clock. Man-made perfection. I am always curious to know how things work, and am keen to add my own contributions when possible. I think that's one of the reasons calendars fascinate me so much.

Modern technology has transformed our interactions with everything around us, from the tools we use to the games we play. I stopped wearing a wristwatch when I started using a mobile phone about 20 years ago, but I quickly discovered that I didn't like having to fish a phone out of my pocket just to see what time it was. So I ended up buying a new watch just for fun, as something to enjoy for its functionality and beauty.

What makes us happy? Apart from all kinds of non-material aspects, I believe there is happiness to be found in the little things: flicking your wrist to see the time on a well-designed watch, or playing a vinyl record instead of an mp3. As far as I'm aware, we are not plugged into a simulated, Matrix-like world. We stand on solid ground and live in relation to one another. The material world connects us. I enjoy touching the things that surround me, to feel, smell, hear, taste, and see. These sensations give me pleasure; they reflect how my body is constructed. They make me feel alive.

Analog and tangible objects like physical calendars are being revived because of our yearning to re-establish contact with the actual, the real, the haptic. Of course a perpetually synchronized digital calendar on your mobile phone can be very useful, but a well-designed physical object – in this case a calendar – can stop you in your tracks. Paradoxically, it can halt time in a way. And time is a component of stress as well as the treasure of our life.

A well-designed calendar can give us insight in to the systems in which we live. It opens our eyes to the fleeting nature of time. It works beyond its initial function as a time keeper to bring us a moment of contemplation. These are the things I had in mind when I created The Cube Calendar. I designed it as a compact object that could subtly change shape in your hands; by tearing off a card each day, you could reveal the workings of time. Every now and then The Cube Calendar reveals a card with a quote about the experience and passing of time. Some are poetic, while others are more practical, to be remembered or filed away for later use.

The best in contemporary calendar design is collected in this publication. You'll find 111 different calendars created by 103 designers and studios from around the globe – reason enough to assume that calendar design is not only alive and well, but flourishing. Let's celebrate this ode to the visualization of time. Long live the calendar!

Philip Stroomberg (b. 1967) is an Amsterdam-based graphic designer who works primarily in the cultural sector. His clients include universities, publishers, and art institutions. Stroomberg regularly creates designs that are used to promote Dutch culture. An important feature of his work is interaction: his designs encourage the user to develop a bond with the object and often challenge the user's imagination.

Chrono-Shredder

Chrono-Shredder celebrated remorse for the lost moment. It was a poetic machine with functions similar to those of a calendar and a clock. Inside the box, the calendar year (printed on a paper roll) was fed through a shredding unit that was controlled by a computer chip. Slowly and continuously the device shredded every single day, minute after minute, hour after hour. After 24 hours one completed day had been destroyed. The tattered remains of the past piled up in the form of paper strips under the device as time passed by.

DESIGN
Davide Ronco

Date (Igenic Calendar)

This calendar, an idea submitted to a contest held by student housing, was made from empty toilet paper rolls. Packaging paper was glued over the end of each roll, giving the calendar a unified appearance while leaving room for notes under each date. The idea was to hide small objects or candies behind the paper and every day break it open to find the object and mark the passage of days. Date was a very simple calendar; it could be created using only toilet paper rolls, and everyone enjoyed filling it with little surprises.

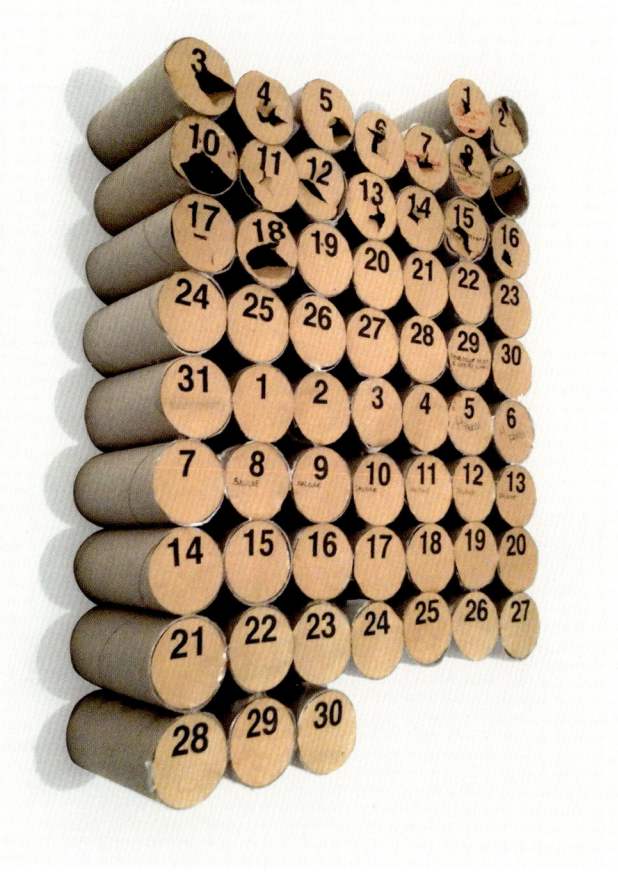

DESIGN
Maude Leclerc-De Guire & Maxime Levesque

Cycle Binaire

Cycle Binaire was made by Maude Leclerc-De Guire and Maxime Levesque. Their goal was to create a calendar which would bring the relationship between users and organizers to another level. Cycle Binaire brought back the basics of simplicity by discarding any identification related to the day or month of the present year. With just a single glance, this calendar could provide a complete retrospective of a year due to its linear grid. Broken down into three geometric forms, the indicators allowed the user to customize their own Cycle Binaire, encouraging common memory practices.

DESIGN
Nitzan Pode

3D Calendar & Dish Dryer Rack, Wooden Engraving

Designer Nitzan Pode turned the rack into a simple set of axis that made it easy to understand the day, the date (Hebrew and Christian), the time, the number of meals she had each day, and the amount of people she dined with. The Y axis measured the amount of people and the time they ate in. The X axis was for the date, measured by date of the week and the month.

DESIGN
Elena Bonanomi & Vincenzo Lanziello

DESIGN AGENCY
jekyll & hyde

CREATIVE DIRECTOR
Marco Molteni & Margherita Monguzzi

See Nothing Calendar

The See Nothing Calendar used 365 dots to mark the 365 days of the year, with an additional seven dots that could be used to represent the days of the week. Only 200 calendars were made, and each was completed by two pins made of epoxy used to mark the date. The pins themselves are as unique as the days in singular lives.

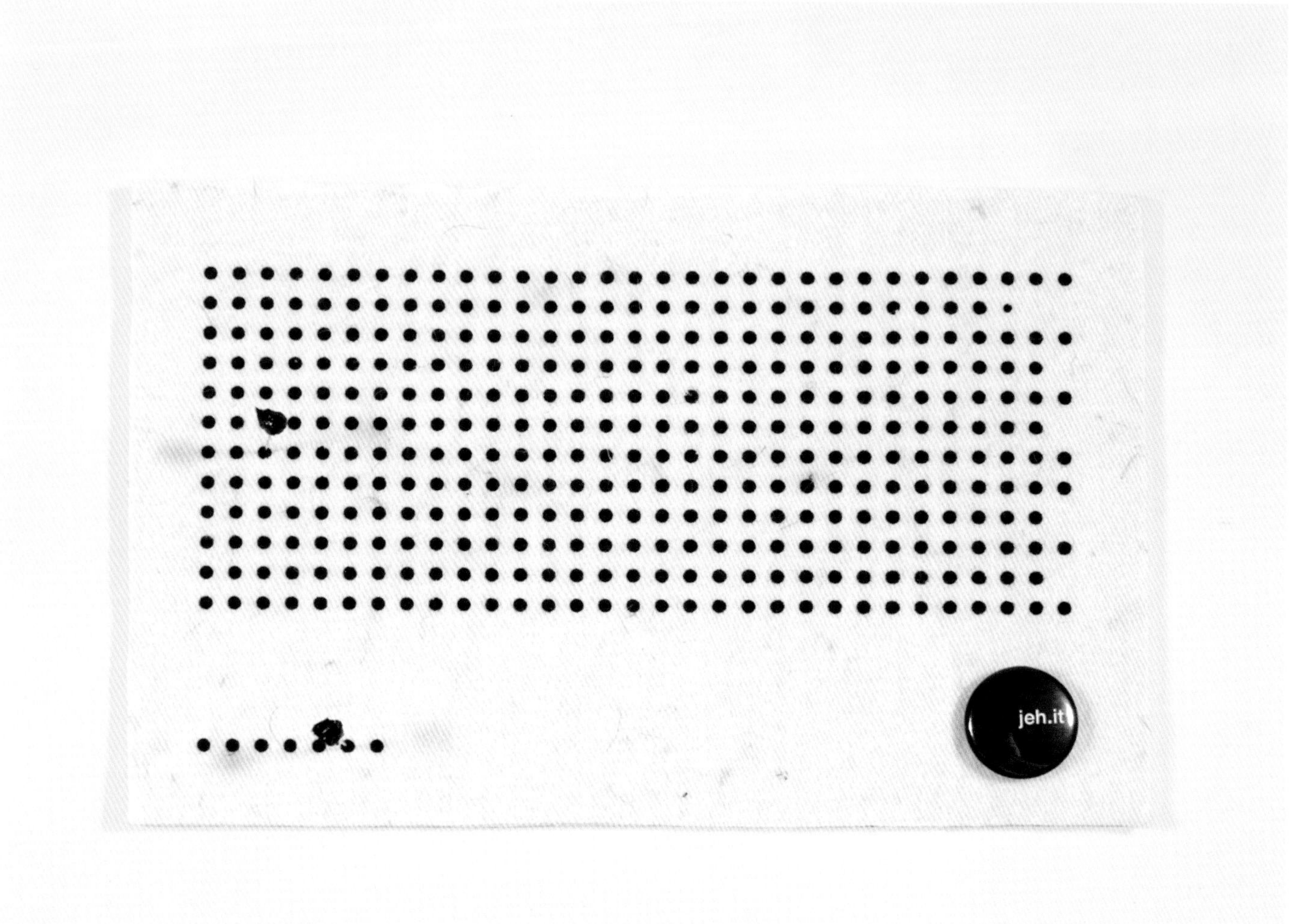

DESIGN
Jared Hansen

PHOTOGRAPHY
Jared Hansen

PROFESSOR
Sohee Kwon

018

2013 Wood Block Calendar

The Wood Block Calendar was a typography class project designed to provide users with a hands-on experience which would fullfil their natural urge to create on a daily basis. The concept behind this calendar stemmed from the designer's memories of using his father's tools to create random projects as a young and creative child growing up. Much like the "random projects" of childhood, this calendar allowed people to create a unique project each month using tools and random objects.

DESIGN
Adrian Westaway & Clara Gaggero Westaway

DESIGN AGENCY
Special Project

PHOTOGRAPHY
Adrian Westaway

Bit Planner

The Bit Calendar is a wall-mounted time planner made entirely from Lego® bricks. By taking a photo of the planner with a smart phone, all of the events and reminders could be synchronized to an online digitalized calendar. It aims to make the most of the tangibility of physical objects as well as the ubiquity of digital platforms. Its power is the immediacy and tactility from the combination of both, and it reveals an immediate overview of how people allocate their time.
Although it uses Lego® bricks, the project is not a Lego® project or endorsed by Lego® in any way.

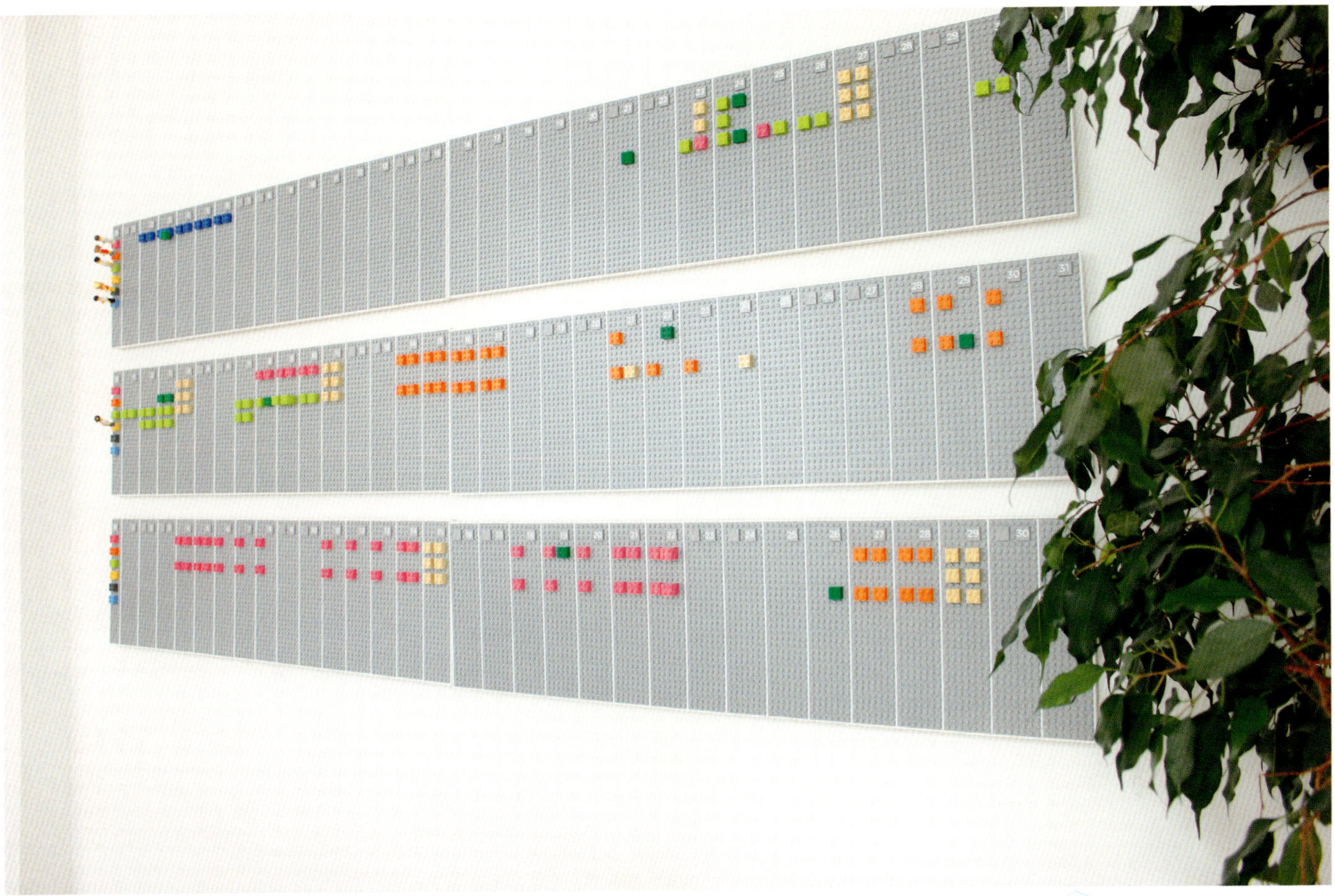

021

DESIGN
Karina Ebner

Christmas Calendar

The Christmas Calendar helps celebrate the month of December by using red elements like paper snowflakes and Christmas-inspired symbols to decorate small treat bags and cards for short messages. The entire calendar was handmade from thin paper and hand-drawn numbers. The separate parts were all gathered together with strings of varying length.

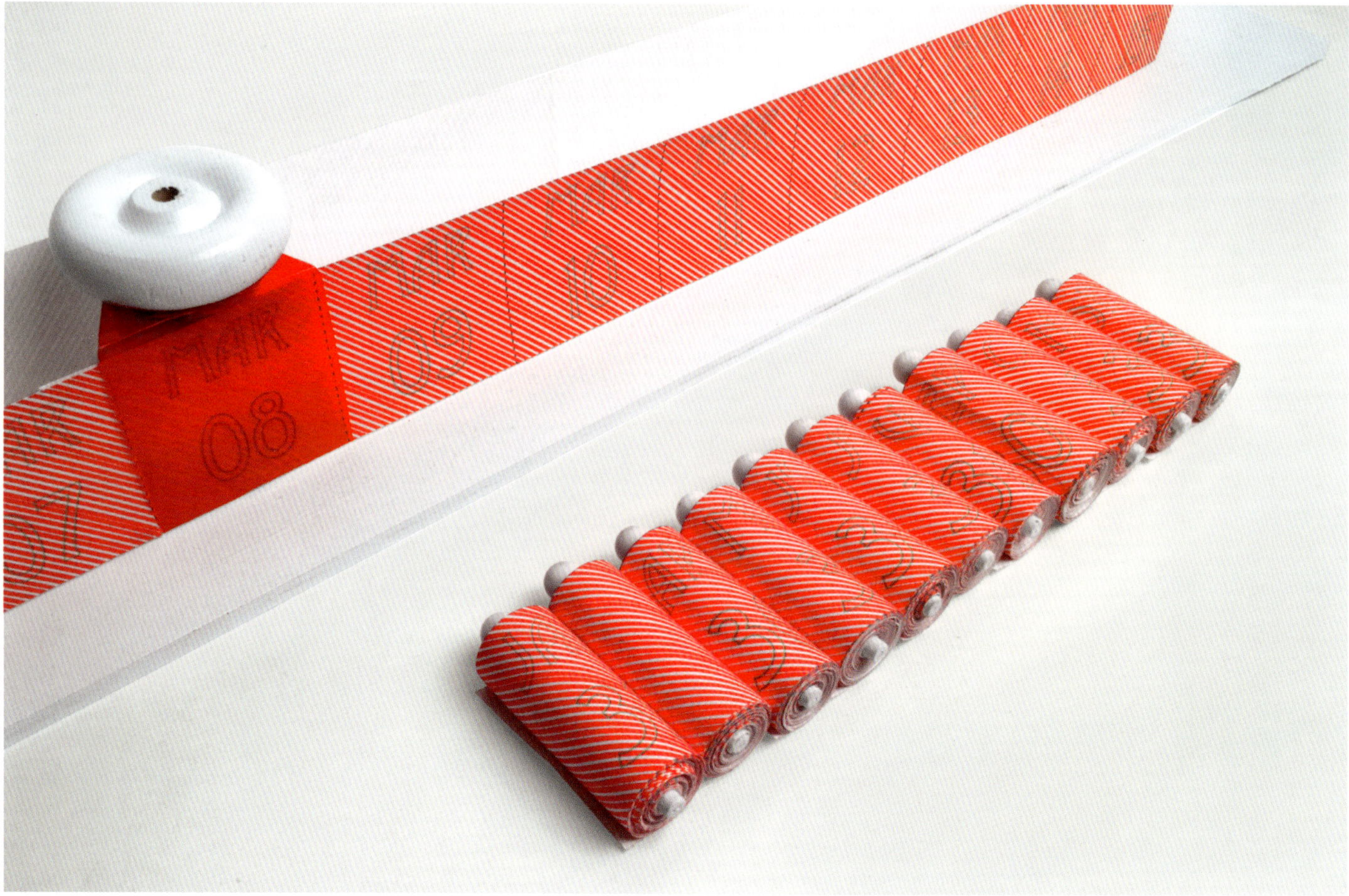

DESIGN
Markie Dossett

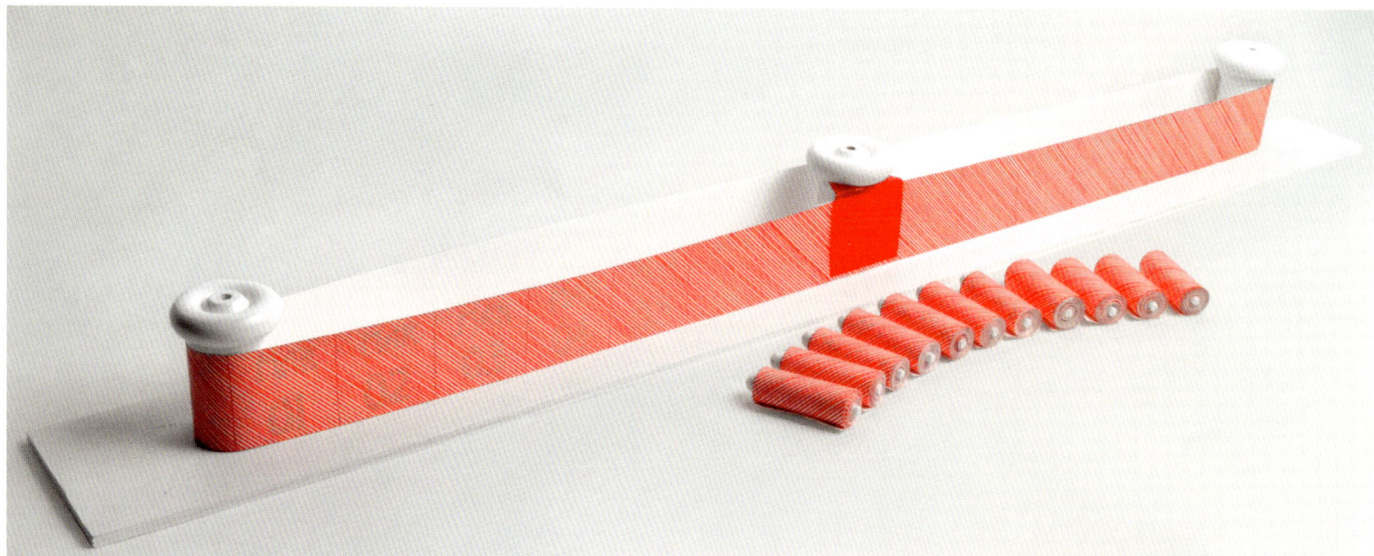

Reveal the Day

This was a nontraditional calendar design created by Markie Dossett. The designer constructed a system consisting of a wooden base, a paper strip containing the month and day, and several knobs for a calendar unlike any other. The wooden base secured the strip, which was guided by knobs that were easily removed for application of the strip itself. Once the strip was placed, people could change the day of the month by turning both end knobs in the same direction. The date would only be revealed when it was aligned with the transparent red film at the center of the calendar. The project resulted in a calendar that was fun and aesthetically pleasing while still functional.

DESIGN
Yael Alkalay

Calendar Design

This calendar design was originally conceived as an experimental typography project. The designer's vision was to create a testament to the beauty and mystery of the notion of time. The handmade quality of the design - created through a process of crafting, printing and photographing - reflected the mystical nature of the perception of time. To produce this concept, designer Yael Alkalay started with a handmade base. She then integrated different shades of light and applied various various techniques and angles. The colors were chosen to evoke the atmosphere of each unique season, and each color was associated with a month. The calendar presented both Gregorian and Hebrew dates, displaying the Hebrew and Latin letters side by side.

Transformable Calendar

As physics says, time is related to space. We're no physicists, but this is still a logical reason for us to create a calendar that works in three dimensions. The elements of the surface of this calendar were designed to have a transformable spatial effect that would go beyond just a wall covering. The designer created it by first creating a raster, then building it with two different materials, one for the triangles and one for the surface they're attached to. The real challenge, however, was to create a product that would function as a calendar but would also have the benefit of being usable after the end of the year; a memory of the entire year that could be displayed in someone's room. The project's final form could be changed and re-arranged to create a new, individually-formed object.

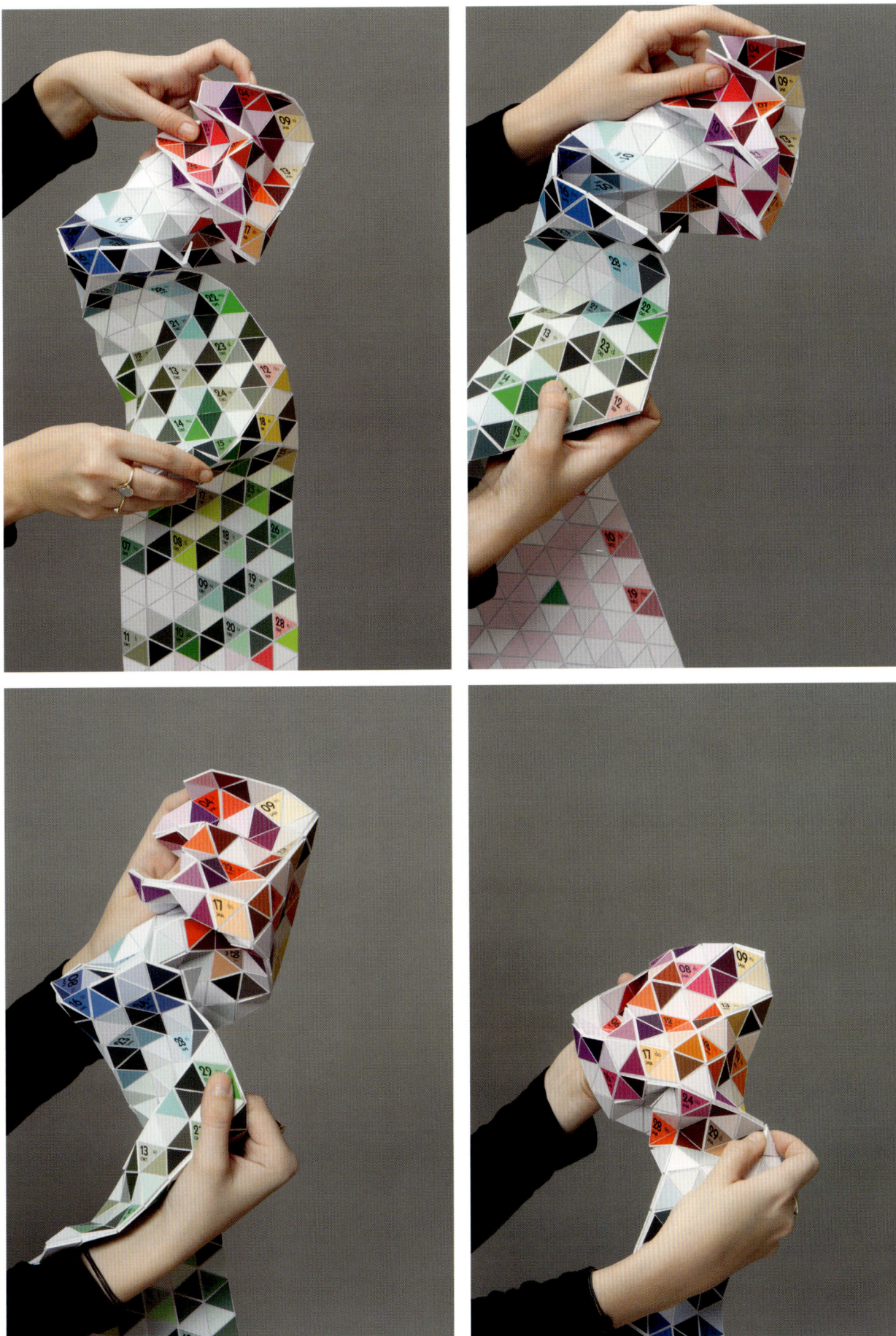

DESIGN
Nikita Kolmogorov

DESIGN AGENCY
StreetArt

PHOTOGRAPHY
Maxim Loskutov

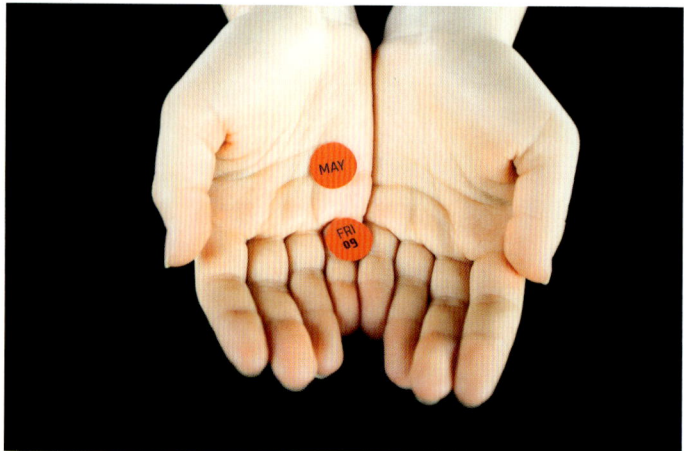

Calendar "Carpe Diem!"

This calendar makes the disappearing, dying year a cause for celebration and a gravestone oration. By trampling on the previous year's grave, one can free themselves from the burdens of the year gone by. The "Carpe Diem!" calendar was designed to be embraced the same way something such as a color, a musical phrase, or a memory would be. To live a "full life," to "live intensely" does not just implying managing to be everywhere on time and being successful, but also to give with everything one's got to give and share without reservation. "Carpe Diem!" is a reflection of this attitude.

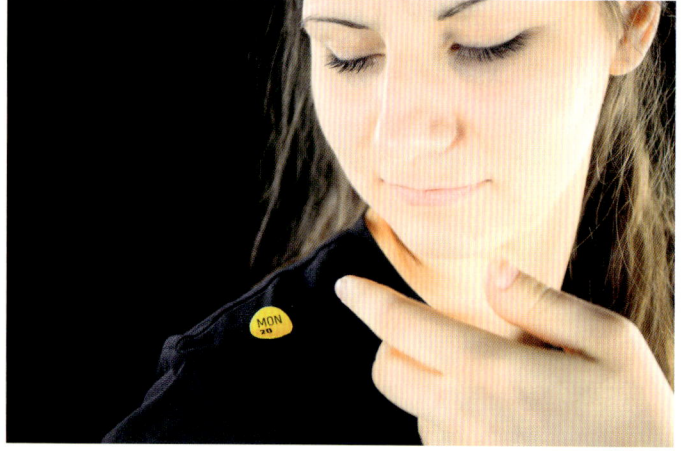

CREATIVE DIRECTOR	PROJECT MANAGER	CONCEPT
Evgeny Fateev	Konstantin Rakhmanov	Maxim Parfenov

DESIGN
Yurko Gutsulyak

ILLUSTRATION
Tatiana Trikoz

CLIENT
JSC Rawenstvo

032

Watching Calendar

People invented calendars to watch time; with this project not only can people watch time but time can watch them as well.

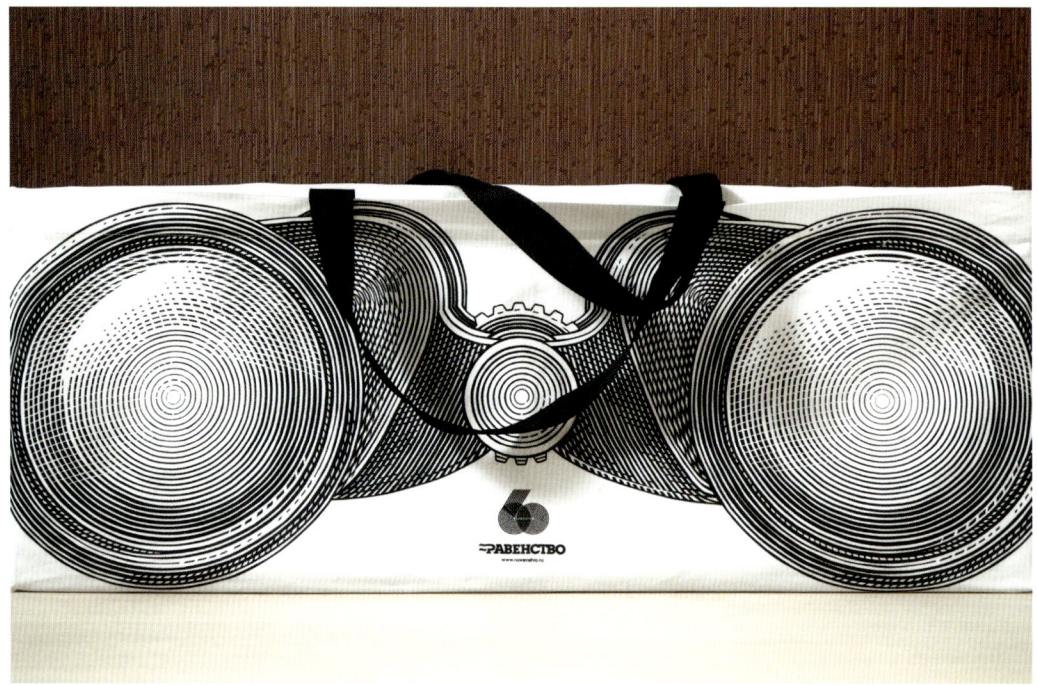

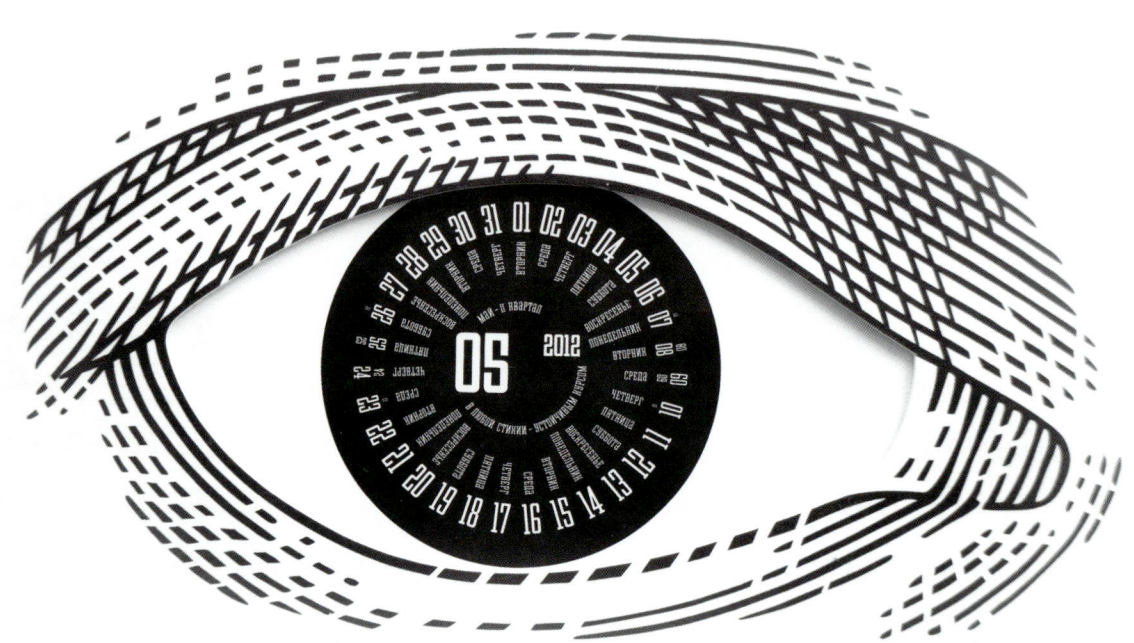

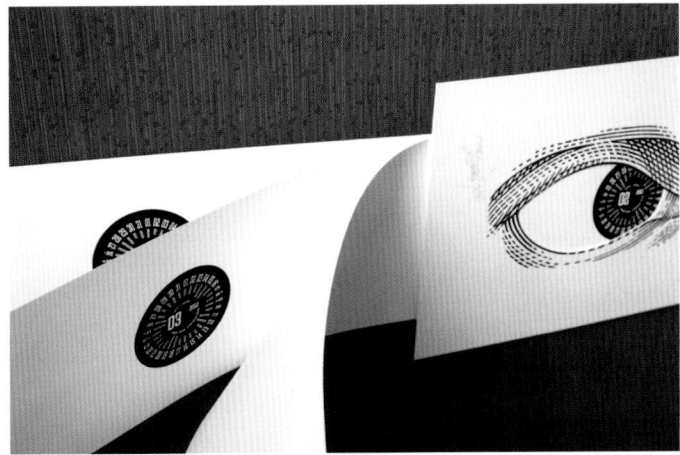

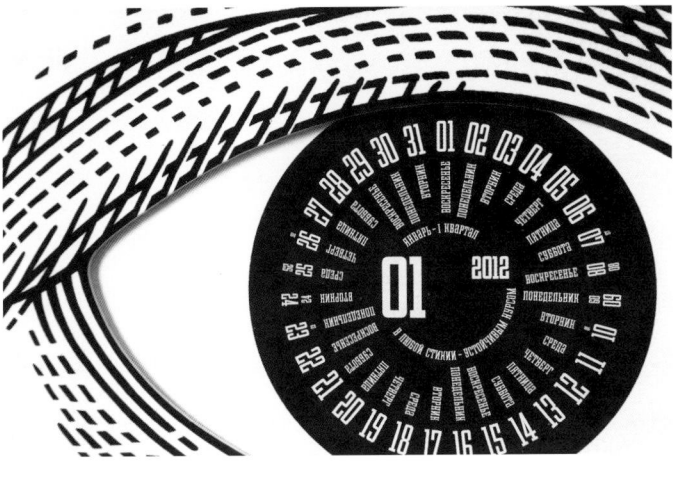

DESIGN
Yurko Gutsulyak

Trash Calendar

Most calendars go immediately into the trash bin when the year is up. This calendar keeps working even in the trash, and reminds people how and why they spend each day.

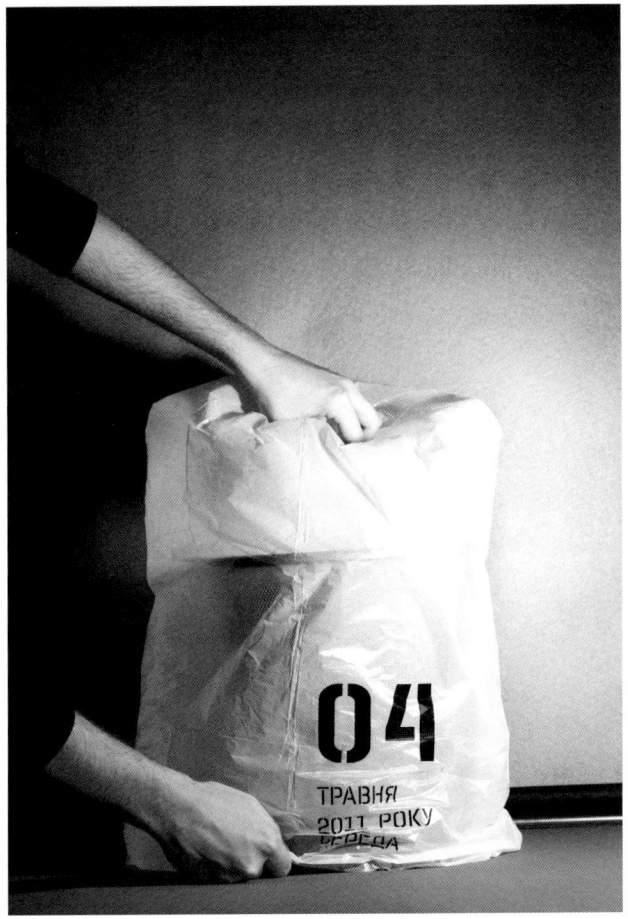

DESIGN
Dina Fiala

PHOTOGRAPHY
Allan Millora Photography

INSTRUCTOR
Dina Vincent

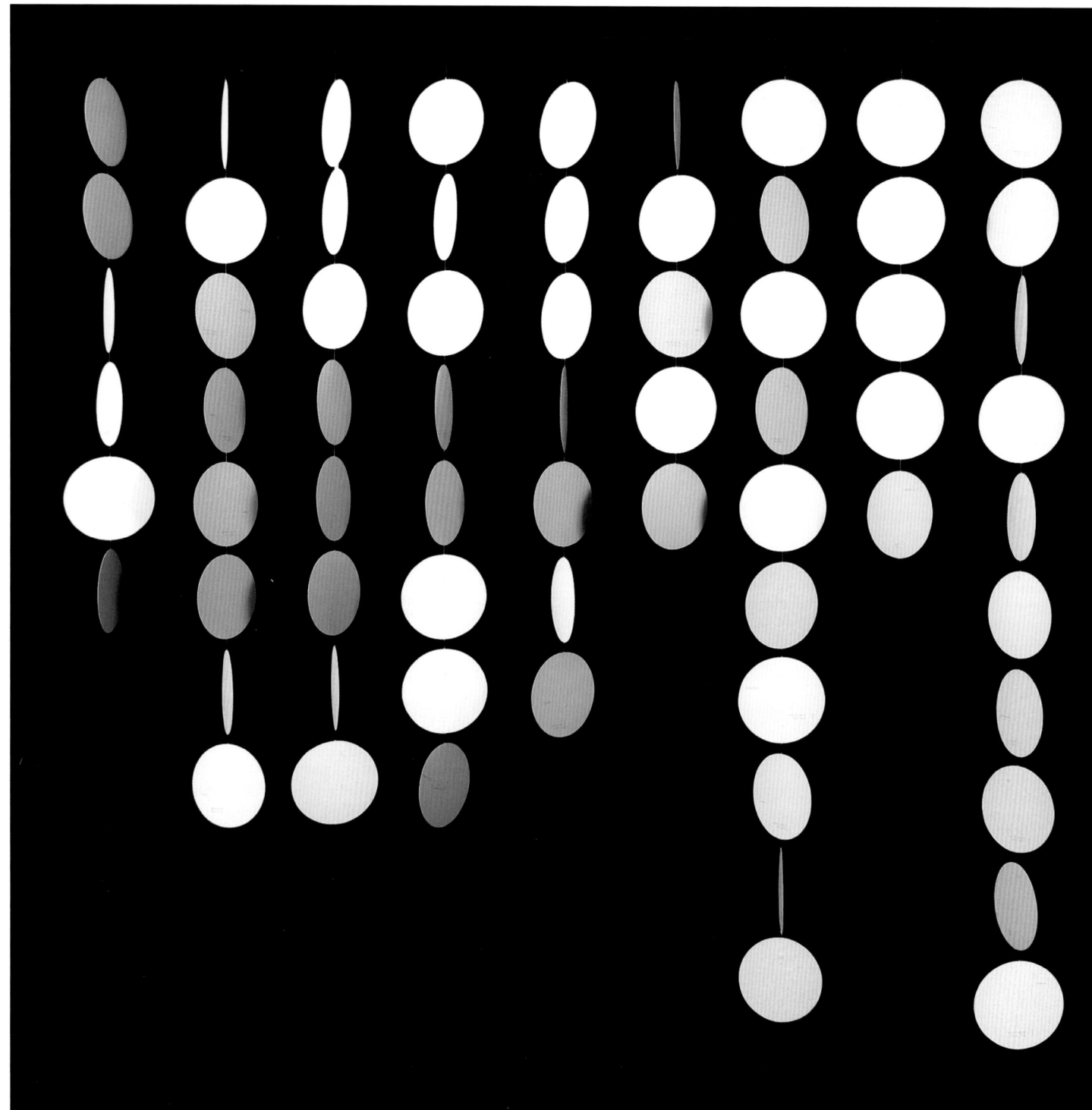

Light Year 2015 Calendar

This project was based on the concepts of "light," "quiet," and "reveal," and was designed to demonstrate the subtle beauty of the stars and moon as they came into the night sky throughout the year. The use of blind embossing and debossing helped achieve the effect of the quiet reveal of the moon and stars. The minimal colors used reinforced the idea of light, and the white on white design evoked the pure beauty of the stars as they revealed themselves in the night sky. The constellations were organized into columns that each represented one month of the Julian calendar. The constellations hang in the month in which they are highest in the sky and best visible from Earth. The reverse side of the discs showed the phases of the moon throughout the year. The discs were hung in a linear fashion along a single plane, and were free to rotate individually. This structure demonstrated the theory of the universe as a single plane which contains many spherical, rotating celestial bodies. The Light Year 2015 Calendar was a project for the Graphic Design Certificate Program made by Dina Fiala when she was in the Division of Continuing Education at the Rhode Island School of Design.

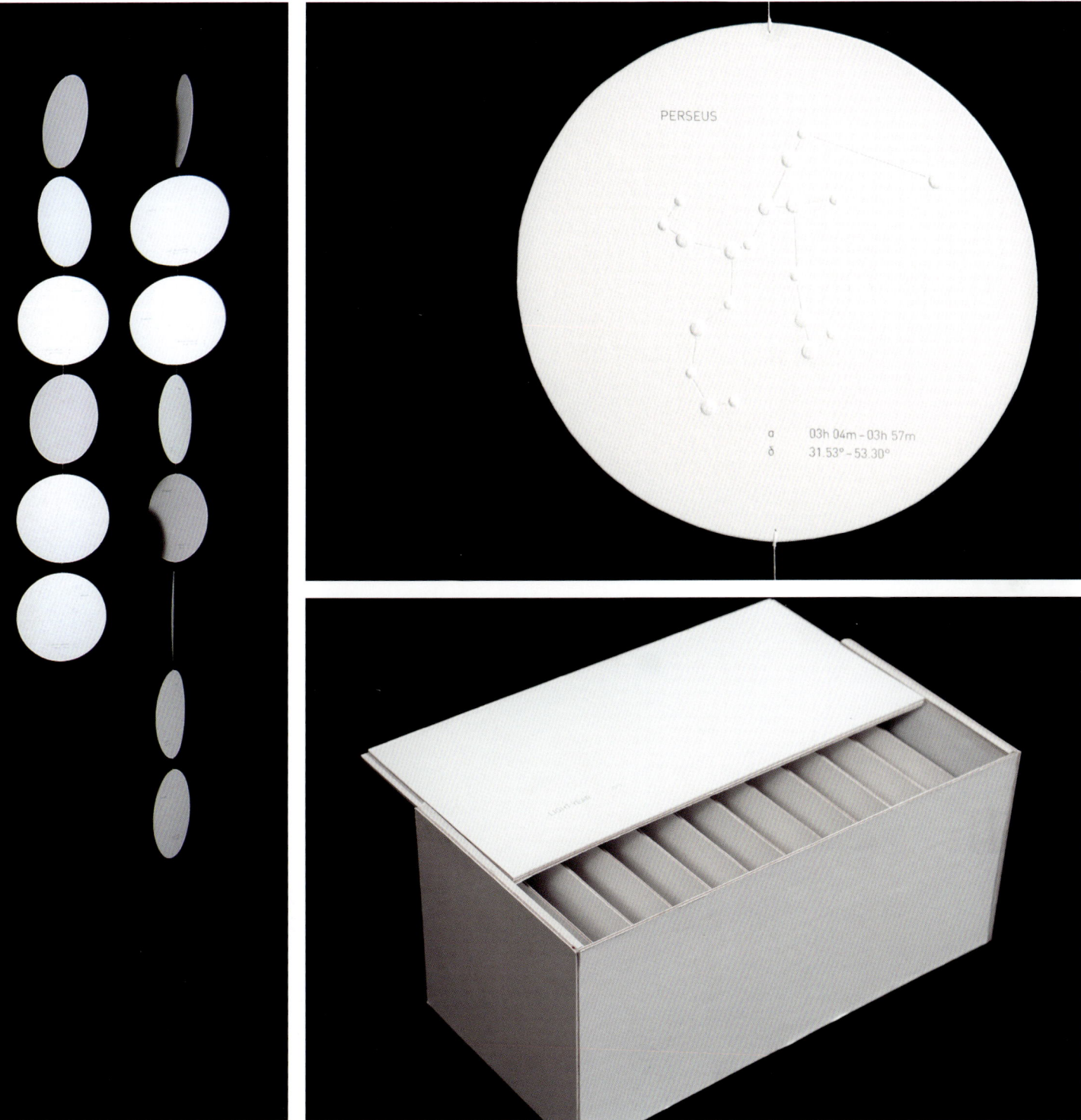

DESIGN
Szani Mészáros

Planet Calendar

Designer Szani Mészáros used different papers for each month and a special case which could be opened as needed for this calendar. As time went by, users could remove the old paper and replace it with the current month. This calendar indicated only some days of a given month, from which users could track the rest of the days as needed.

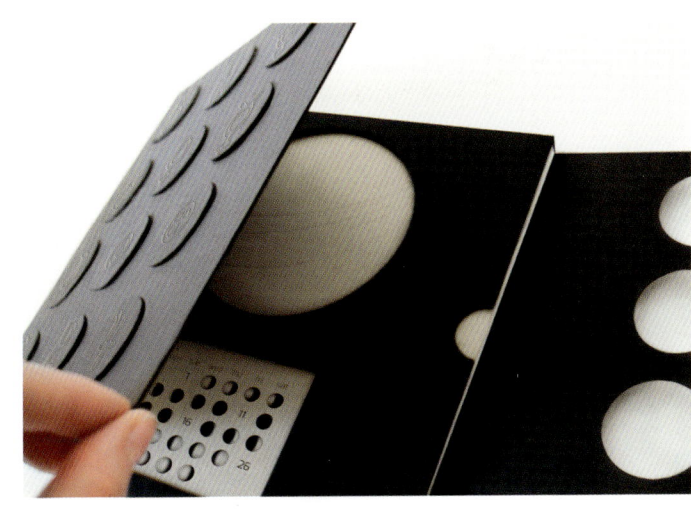

DESIGN
Eszter Varga

Calendar

This calendar consisted of 16 pages and was constructed in the form of a pyramid. The different graphic logos each represent different seasons.

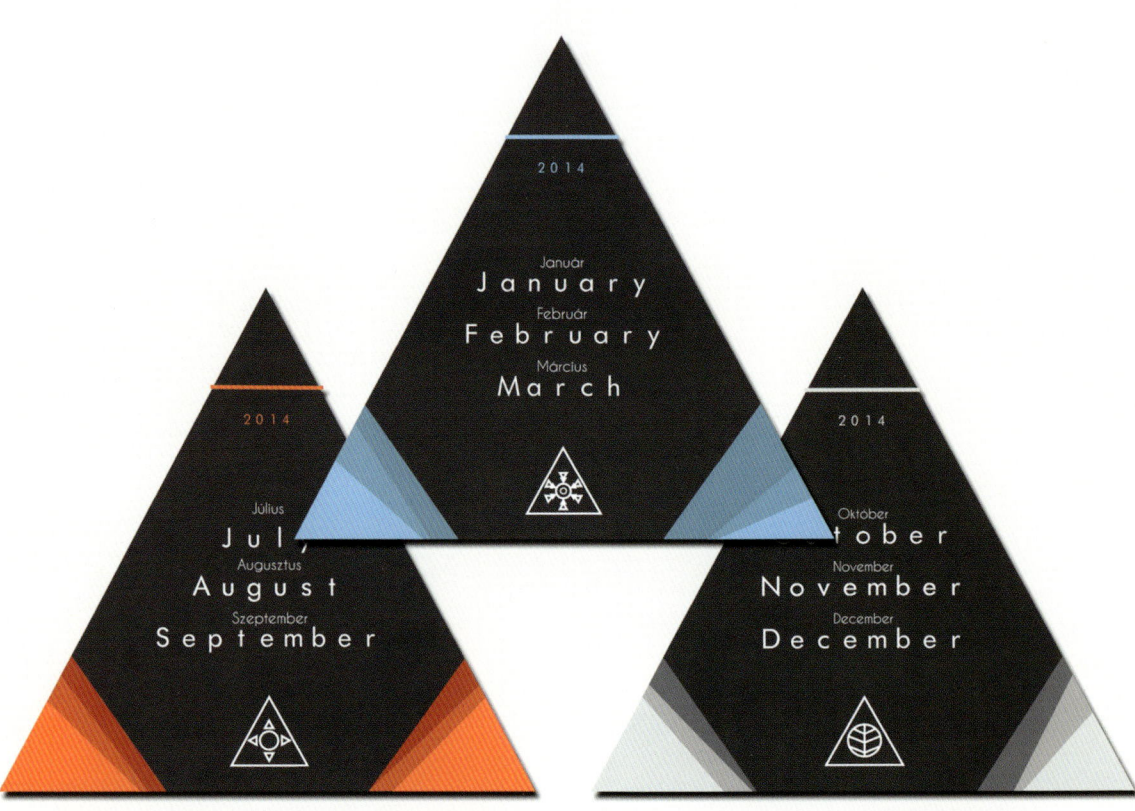

DESIGN
Lucia Freire Coloma

1m. Tear off Calendar

The starting point of this project was a reflection about the measurement of time; therefore, designer Lucia Freire Coloma designed a vertical 1m long calendar that mimicked a measuring tape. Every day people tore off a piece of the calendar, and as the month shrunk, it showed a background with the color of the season and the sentence "As time goes by…" to reinforce the concept.

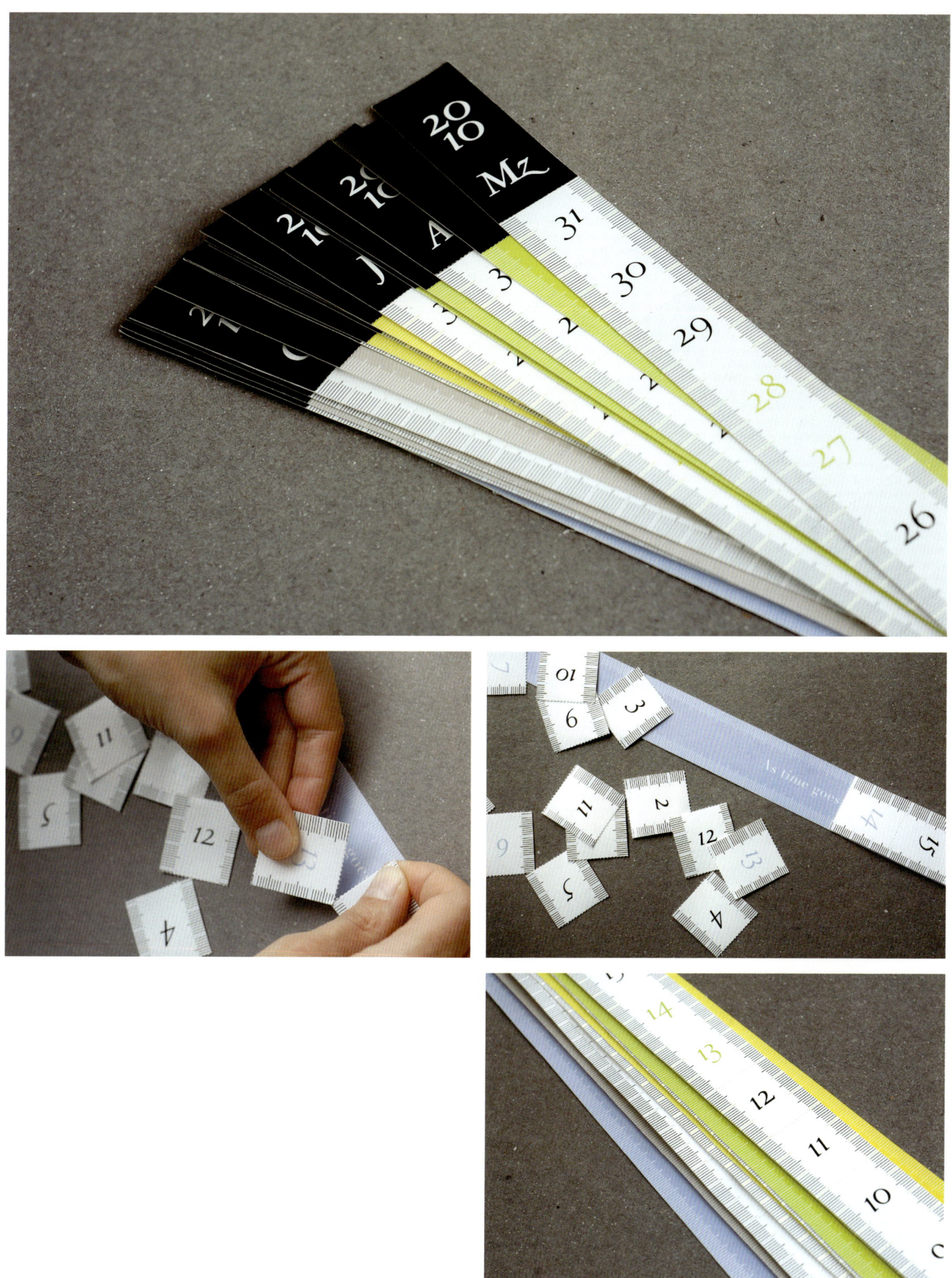

DESIGN AGENCY
Kolle Rebbe

CLIENT
Hälssen & Lyon

The Tea Calendar

The Hälssen & Lyon was the first calendar with days made from tea leaves. Thanks to an entirely new manufacturing process that made each of the 365 days out of tea, each could be individually detached and brewed in hot water like regular tea. Hälssen & Lyon's customers, suppliers, and business partners who received the tea calendar could enjoy the authentic taste of the innovative and diverse tea products from the company. Each calendar day proved that the company was one of the most innovative tea manufacturers in the world.

DESIGN Tom Davall
PHOTOGRAPHY Julie Brock

Weather

Chinese astronomers developed a 24 section calendar which allowed them to predict the weather. When designer Tom Davall decided to research into these different methods of weather prediction he discovered that fortune cookies, tea leaf reading, and tarot cards were amongst them. To present the 24 sections, Tom created this special cup and saucer, replacing symbols normally found on tea leaf reading saucers with set of symbols referring to each section of the calendar.

DESIGN
Philip Stroomberg

PRINTING
Drukgoed & paardekooper

CARDBOARD
IGEPA Nederland

The Cube Calendar

The Cube Calendar adds an innovative twist to the concept of the tear-off calendar. Inspired by thoughts about time, it is a compact object that gradually changes shape: by tearing off a card each day, the user reveals the workings of time. Divided into six rows, hundreds of cardboard cards line up, held together as a cube by two binding screws. The cards have been punched from two sheets of cardboard. There's a card for each day and, every few days, a card with a quote about time – a humorous observation or a philosophical aphorism. The Cube Calendar comes in a specially designed box that folds around the cube without glue or other adhesive. When you lift the lid, the box falls open like origami, leaving the calendar to be picked up. Put four boxes side by side, and you'll get the name The Cube Calendar.

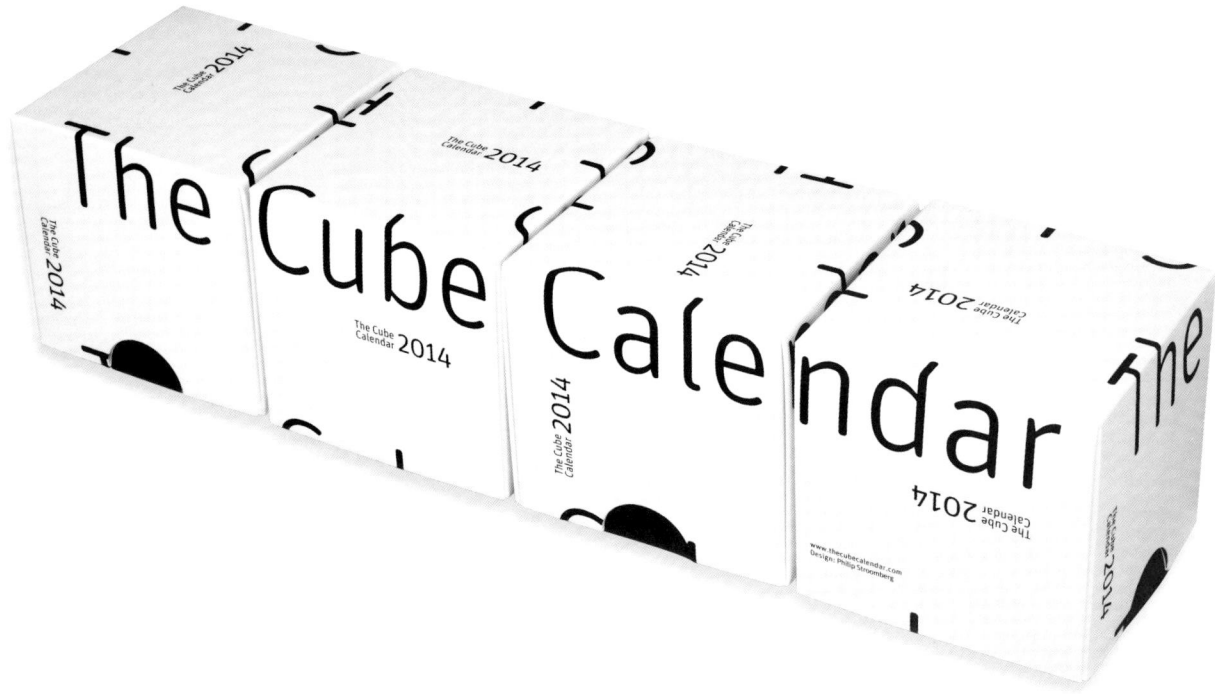

DESIGN
Sebastian Bergne

Monthly Measure

Monthly Measure was both a monthly universal calendar and a ruler. The star could be positioned on the serrated side of the ruler to show the day of the month and the date. The date could be easily changed by rolling the star along the ruler. The dates were placed every centimeter so Monthly Measure could also be used as a metric ruler.

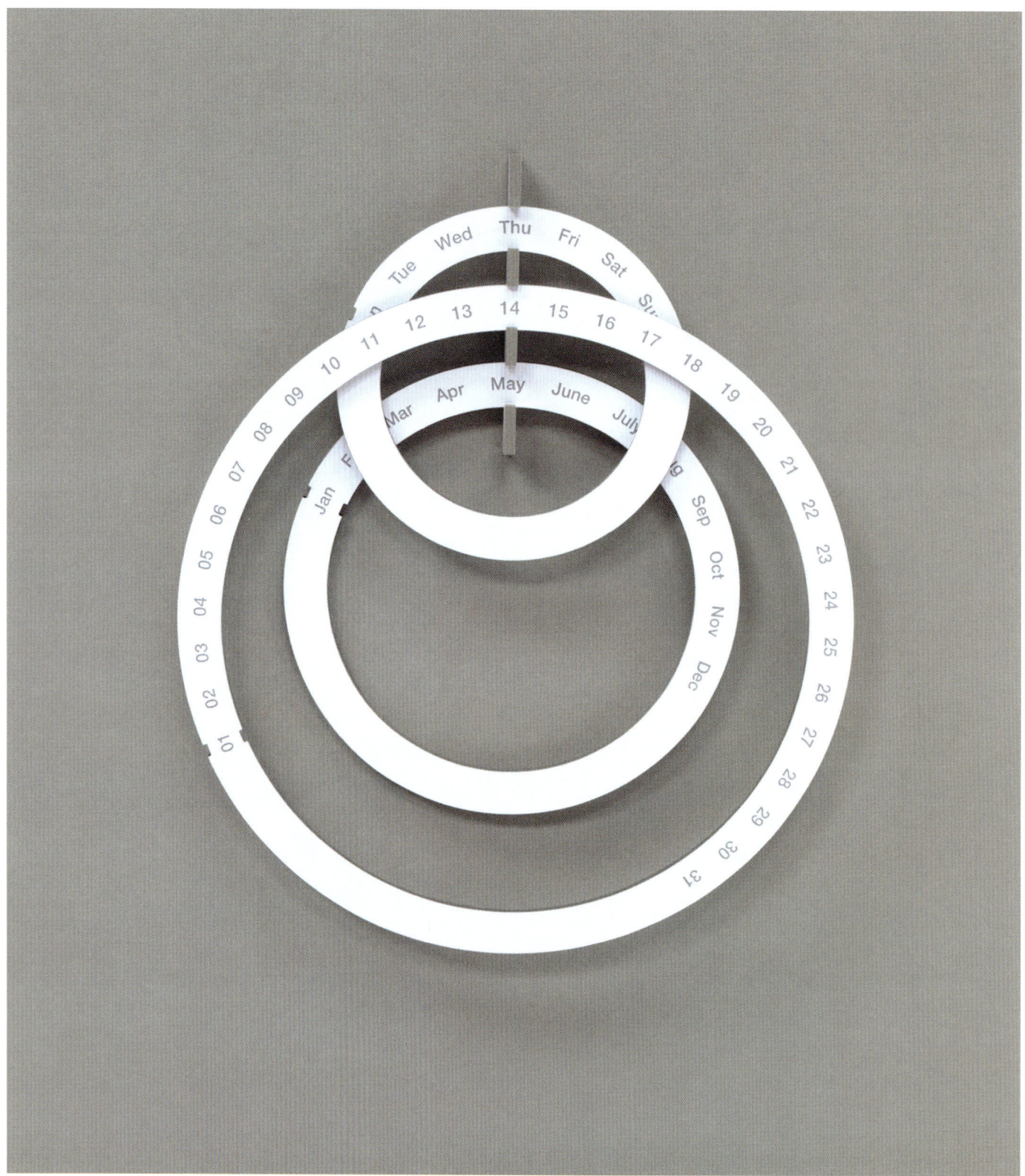

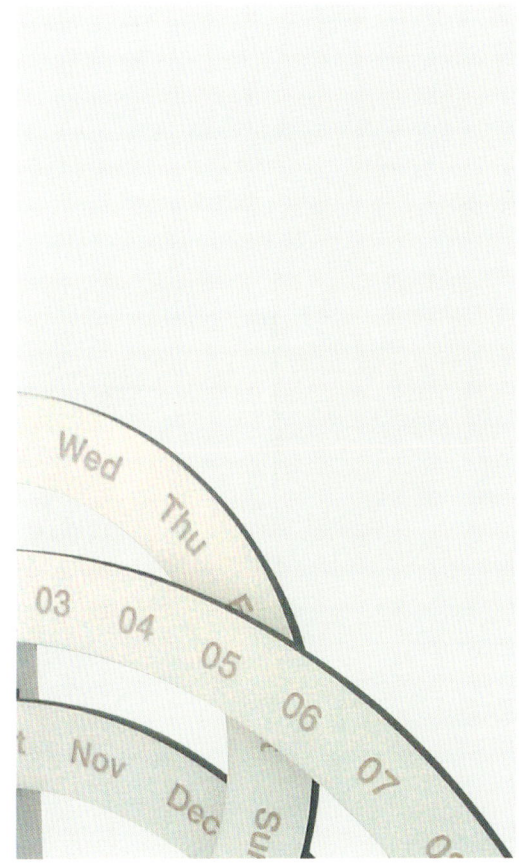
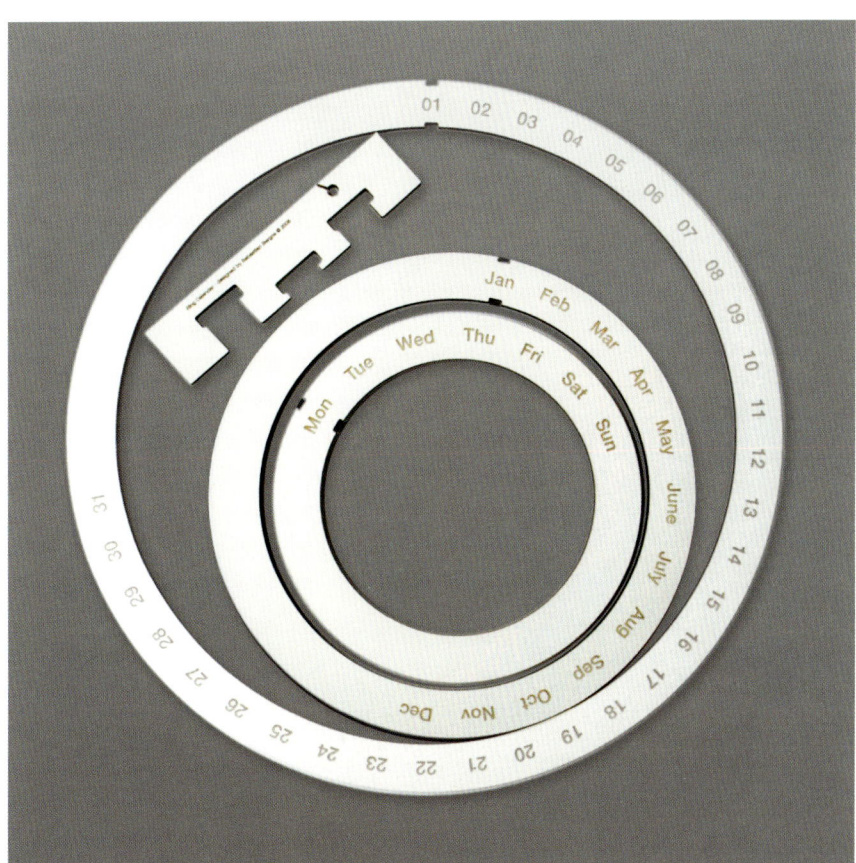
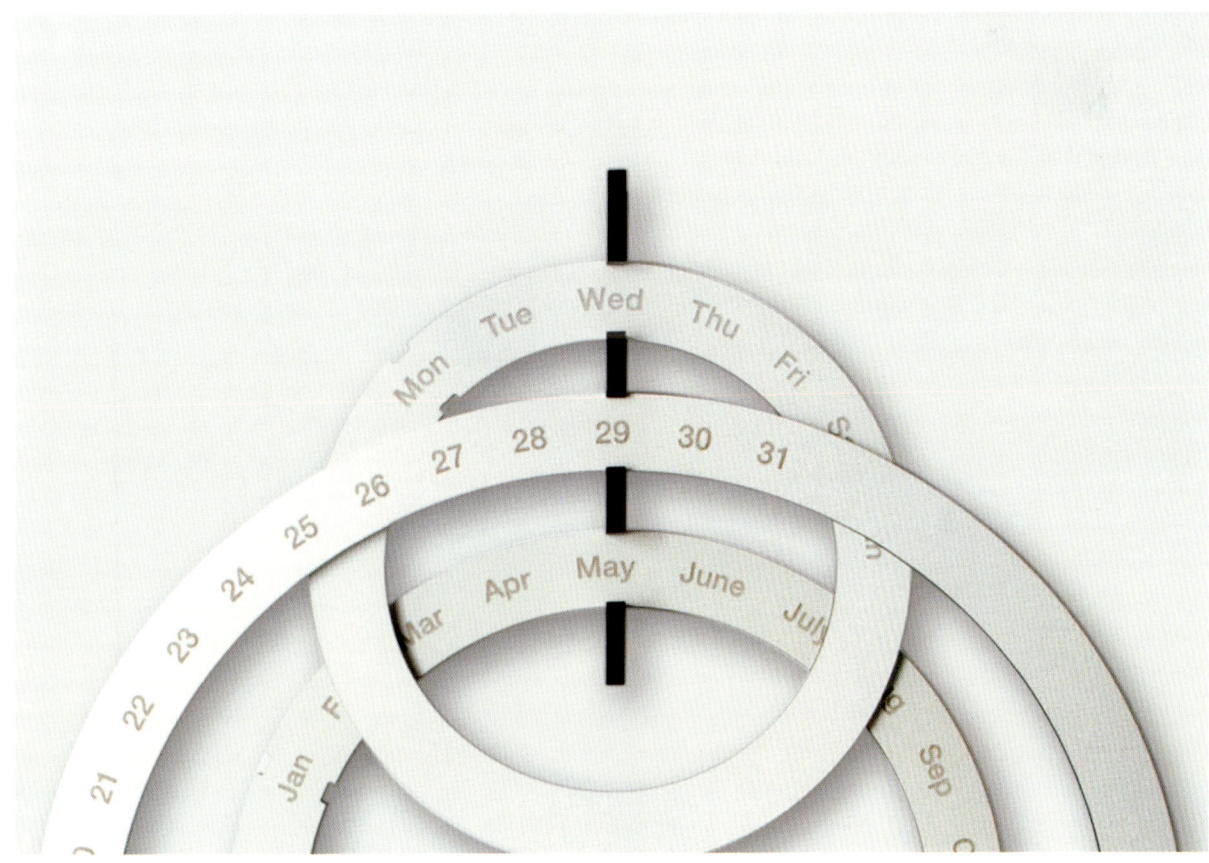

DESIGN
Sumit Vashisth

PRODUCTION DESIGN
Rajesh Bhargava

FABRICATION AND PRODUCTION
DI Concepts

Skyscraper Calendar

This calendar was designed for KRRISH, a construction and real estate firm. The objective was to establish the brand identity through a well-crafted design, and to build stronger relationships with prospective associates. Designers gave life to a simple paper calendar by crafting it into a set of 4 innovative tabletop skyscrapers. This Skyscraper Calendar portrayed KRRISH as a contemporary and innovative brand in cluttered market space. It found its place on the tables of famous architects, associate business firms, and prospective clients.

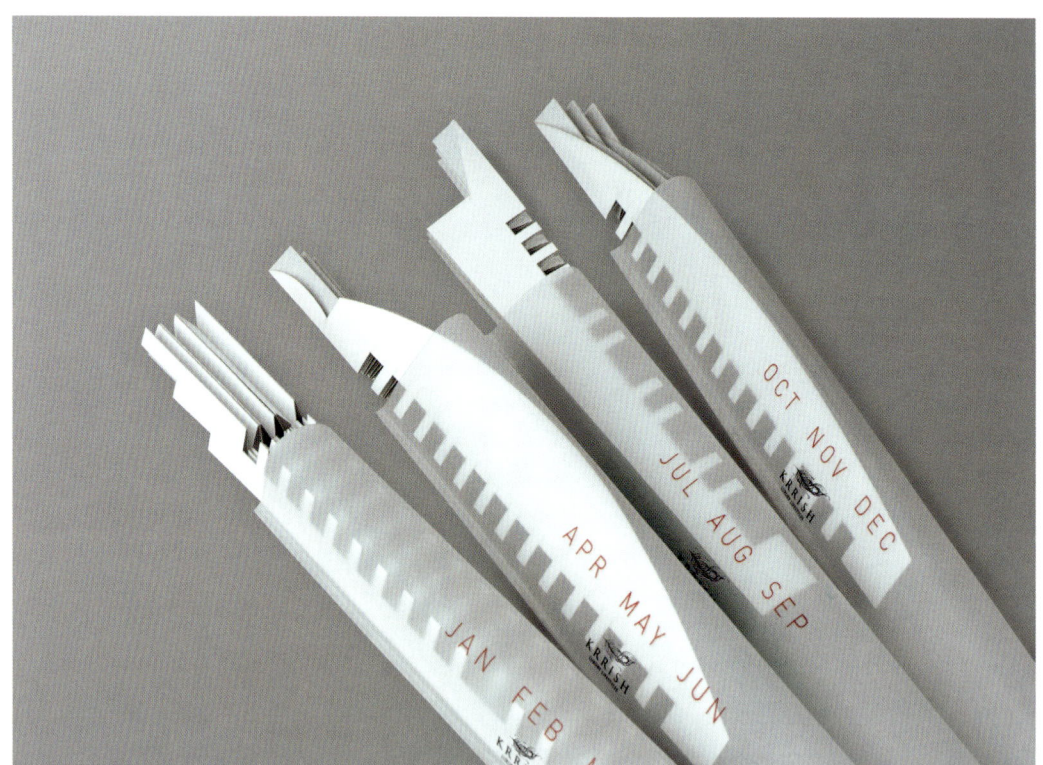

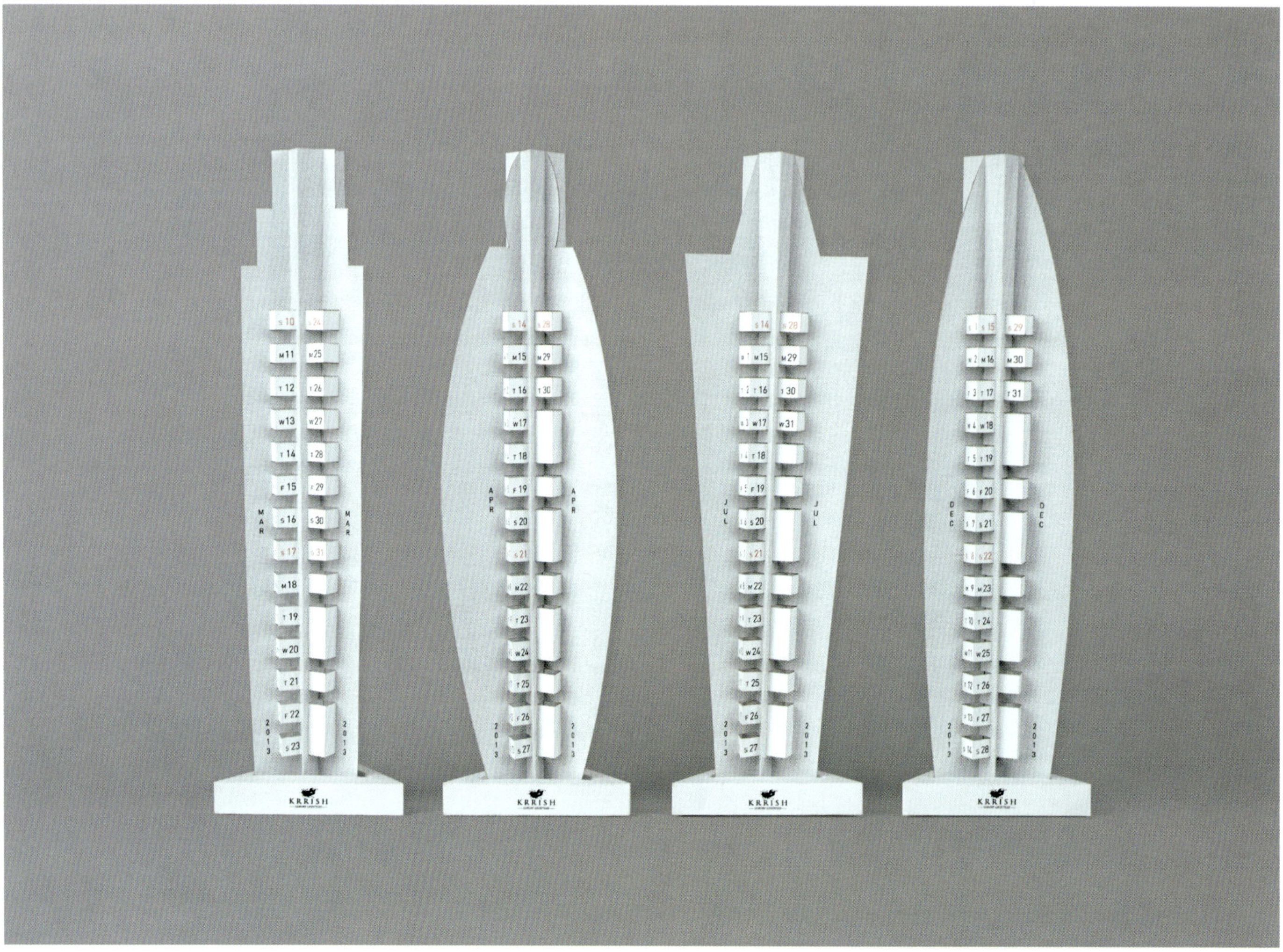

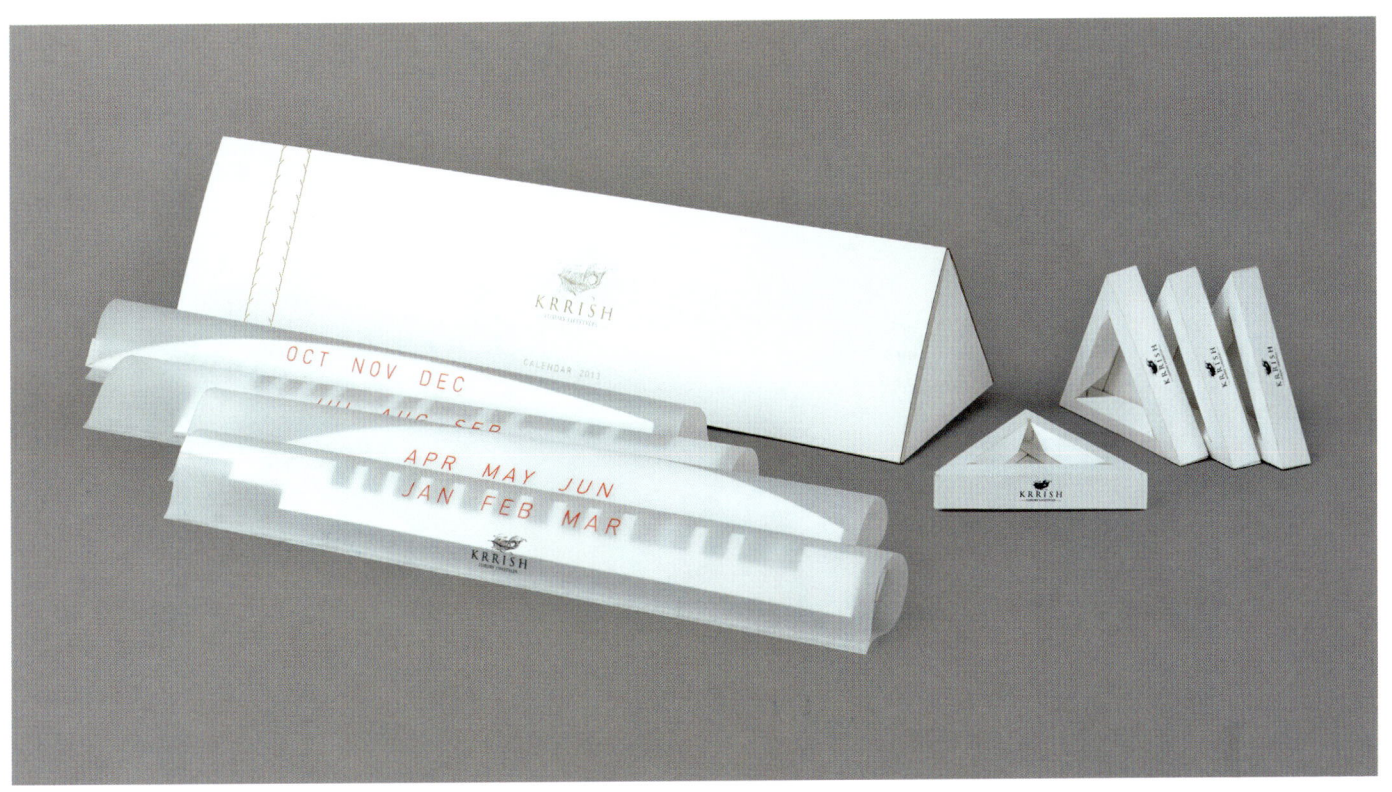
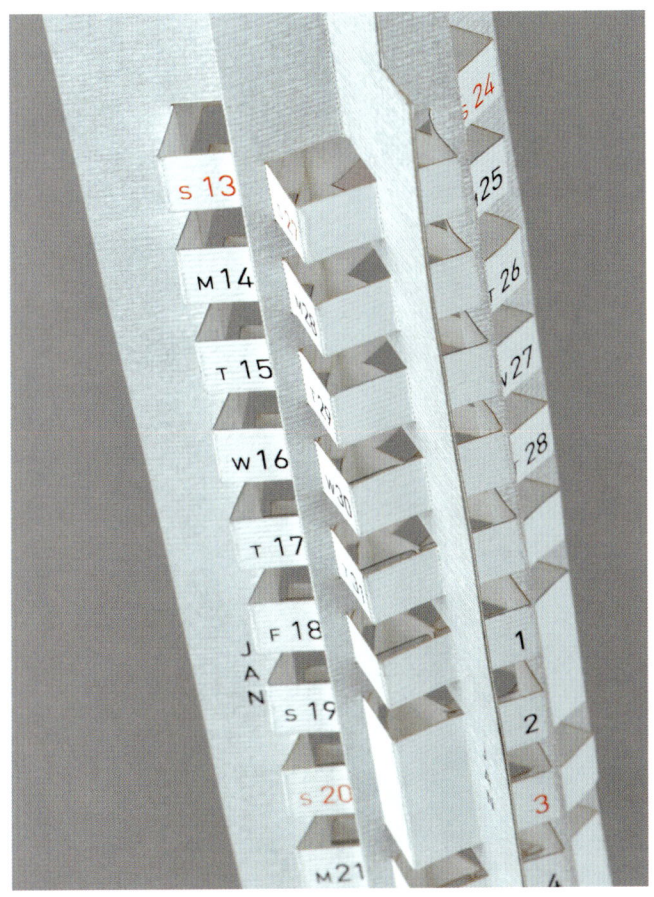
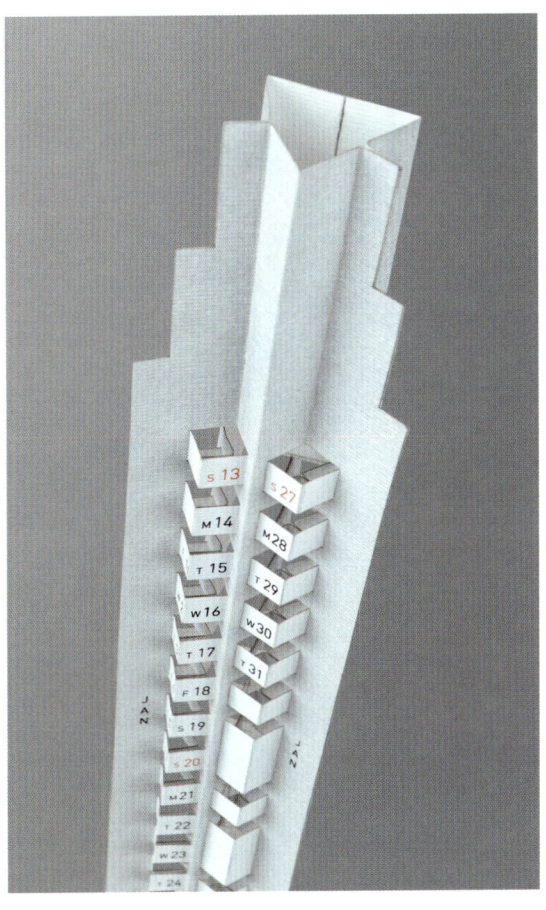

DESIGN
Jodia Steenkamp

30x12 Exposé

The 30x12 Exposé challenged the traditional approaches of calendar design by using a visible, clear, and effective way finding system to contain collected data. To operate the calendar, one would need Pack 1, Pack 2, the 30x12 Exposé App (for IOS and Android), and direct natural sunlight. Pack 1 included a sunbed, sunbed stand, instruction booklet, concertina filing and flash cards. Pack 2 included sundials within their trays and time capsules. Every month, the user would unpack the current month's photosensitive sundials and insert them into the sunbed's delegate color-coded slots. When the sundials were exposed by removing the protective sealant and elevating their gnomon, they documented the weather on the photosensitive paper. At year's end the sundials became part of a huge art piece put together by NASA. Due to the sun's high energy and the sundials' sensitivity, the user had to turn the sundial upside down in its slot on the sunbed to stop the exposure as well as to see the date of the lunar month. The final step in operating was to place each sundial in its delegated time capsule for each month to truly fix the exposure of the sundials.

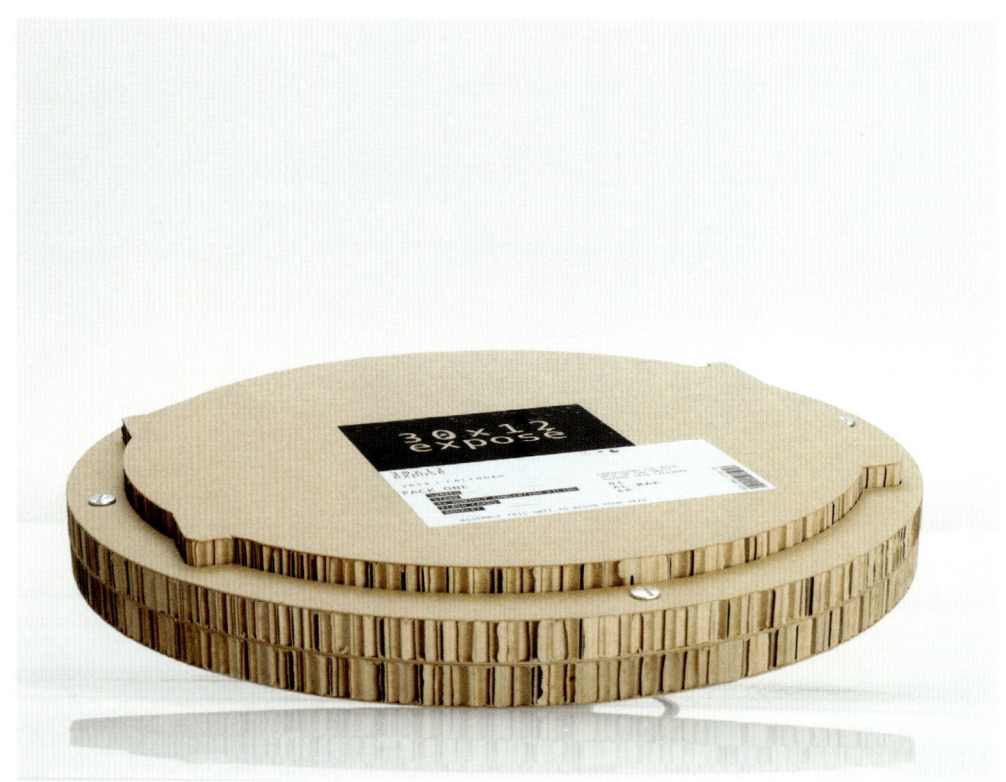

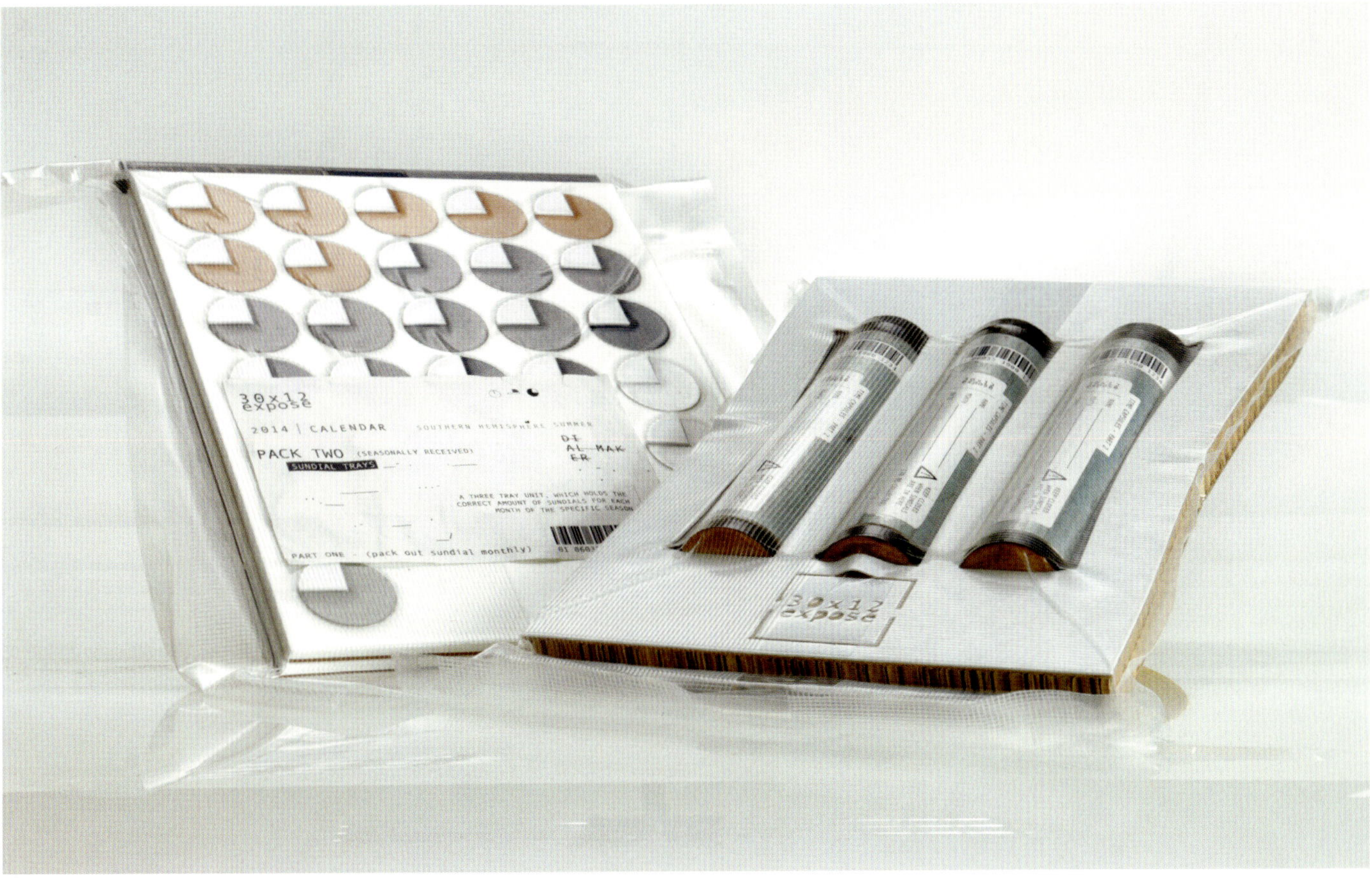

055

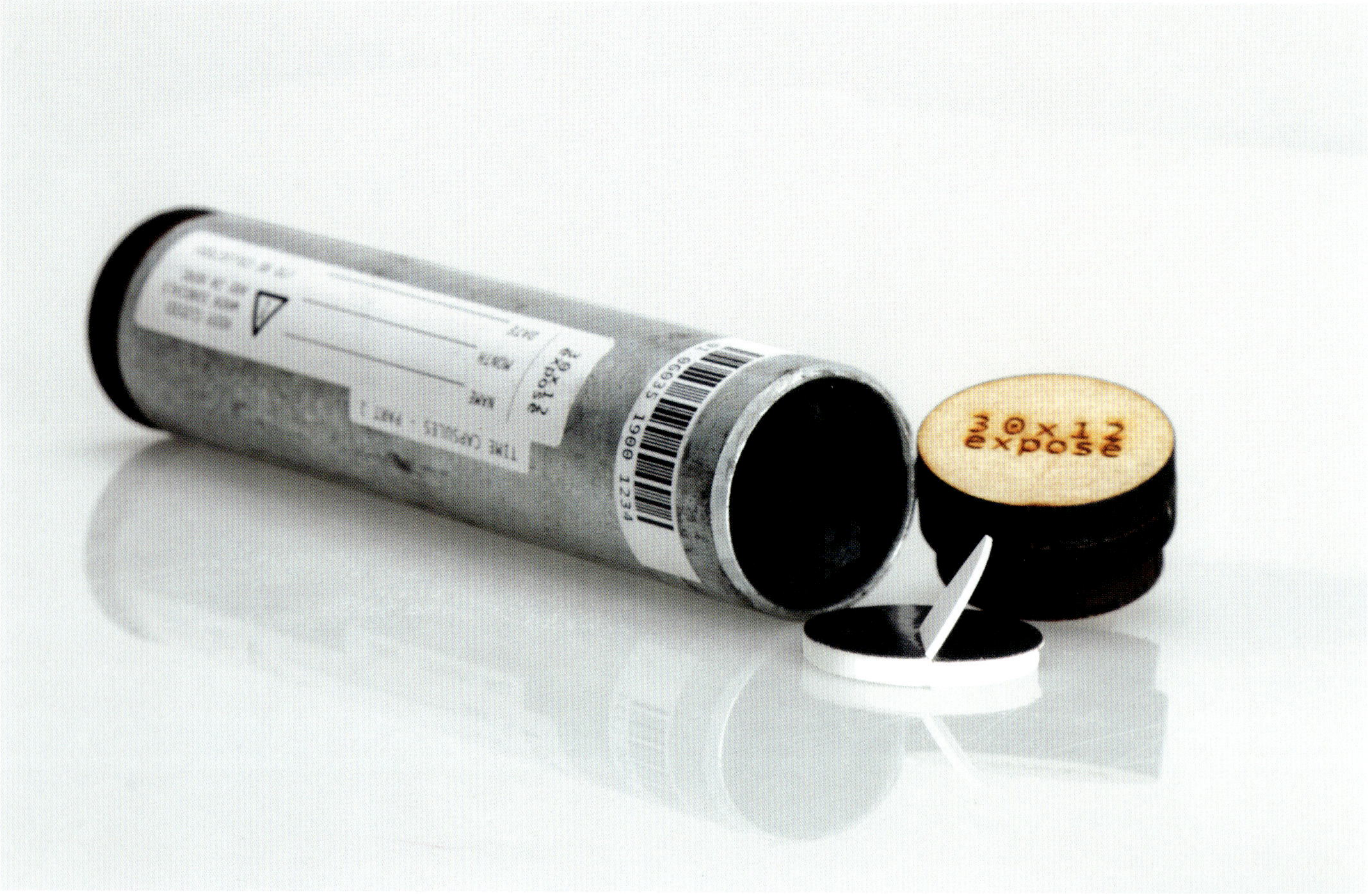

DESIGN
Gideon Dagan

MoMA Perpetual Calendar

MoMA Perpetual Calendar was designed for the Museum of Modern Art, NY. This unique calendar could be used year after year, making it an eco-conscious product. The calendar could be placed on a desktop or mounted on a wall. Its string-tethered ball was suspended in mid-air and was manually moved to mark each month. A second ball on the horizontal beam indicated the day. The calendar was constructed of injected-molded ABS recyclable polymer and magnets. The new mini calendar design commemorated the 10th anniversary of the original design that debuted in 2000.

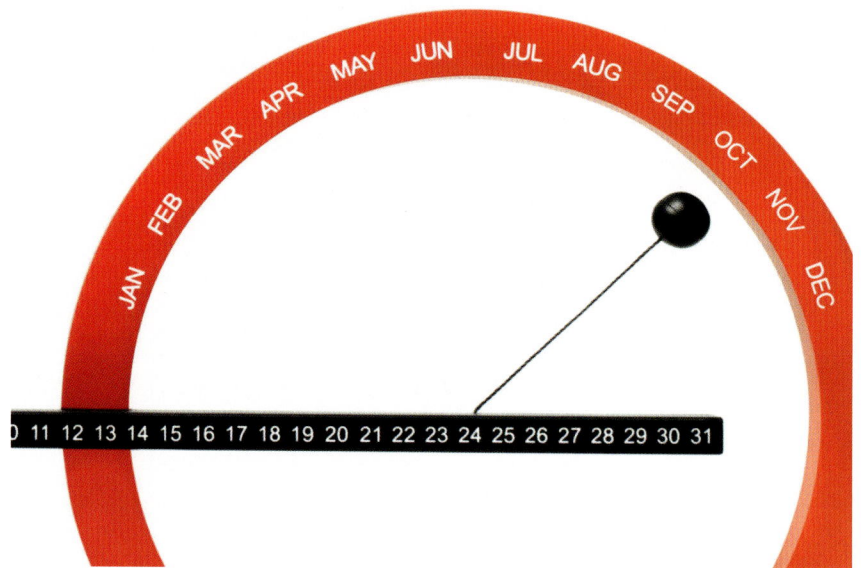

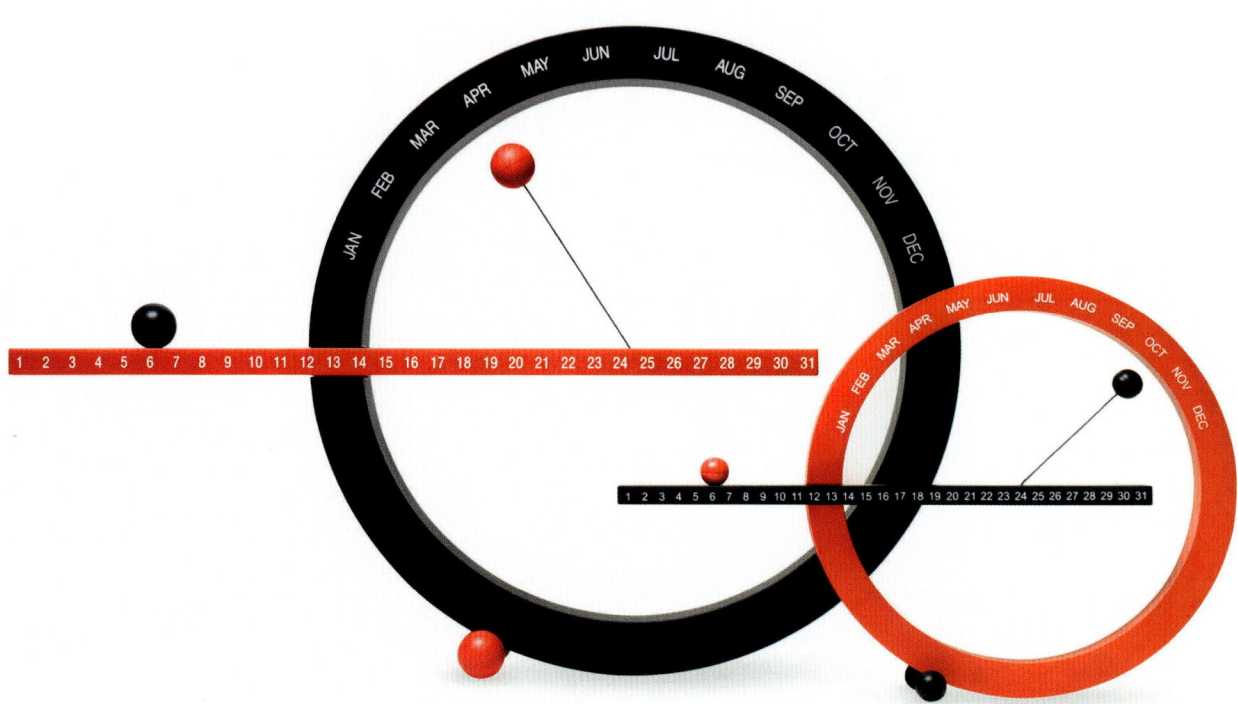

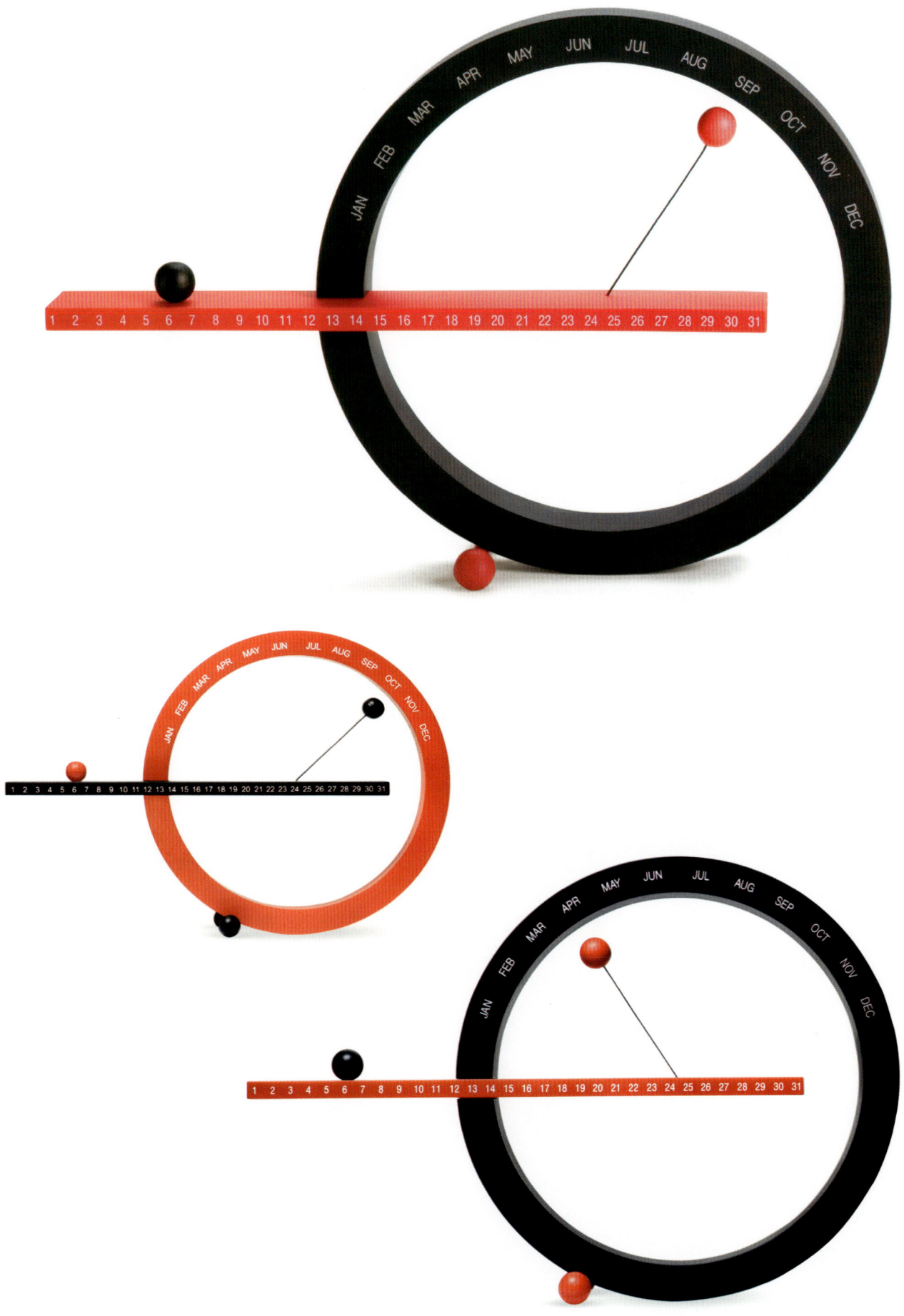

DESIGN AGENCY
TBWA/ISTANBUL

Land Rover Topographic Calendar

Design agency TBWA/ISTANBUL designed a daily 2014 calendar that reflected the off-road spirit of Land Rover by creating a 3D version of classical, flat topographic maps. Colors on each level represented different months and the numbers on the side of each page showed the remaining days of the year.

DESIGN
Chanel Stracey

YCN Competition Fedrigoni Desktop Calendar 2015

An idea playing on the notion of having tea and biscuits at your desk. Chanel Stracey designed a calendar based on a biscuit sampler box, with twelve biscuits to showcase each month. The majority of colors and weights from Fedrigoni's Woodstock paper range are represented. Keeping in theme with the sampler box concept, Chanel recreated a plastic mould to hold the biscuits, an information slip identifying the color and weight of each biscuit, and a cover sheet to protect the biscuits, made from the thinnest paper weight in the range.

DESIGN
Liat Meadows

ILLUSTRATION
Liat Meadows

064

'70s Rock Calendar

Inspired by Great Britain's legendary '70s rock bands, designer Liat Meadows created a vinyl record-shaped calendar that could be turned from one month to another. In addition, the designer also created a pocket calendar designed as a CD case. Each month featured illustrations of a rock band from this era.

Calendar Transformer Kit 2014

The Calendar Transformer Kit consisted of 12 square cardboard modules of different colors which could be combined in a variety of different ways. All of the numbers and letters on the calendar were hand printed. Calendar Transformer was an interactive object that also made an excellent toy for children.

DESIGN
Seoungkyeong Lee

2015 Fedrigoni Calendar

The challenge for this Fedrigoni calendar was to combine a hot beverage sleeve and calendar, and allow designers to do two different things at the same time while working at their desk. Apparently time management is very important to designers -- this calendar serves as a useful tool for those designers who are always forgetting to check their schedule. The calendar can be continuously reused due to the high quality of Fedrigoni's Woodstock paper.

DESIGN
Niels Kjeldsen

Corian Calendar

A tabletop calendar that allows users to enjoy touching Corain's unique material and experience its luxurious surface, weight, and general high quality through its use. The calendar was composed of 12 monthly pieces in different colors, two date cubes, and a solid base. The date could be adjusted by turning the cubes, and the month changed by placing the relevant month in the groove in front of the date cubes. Because the calendar didn't use the names of the days, it could be used forever.

DESIGN
Patrick Florville

Year'Round Perpetual Calendars

Year'Round Perpetual Calendars have been sold in high-end stores worldwide, and these user-friendly, injection-molded calendars are also part of the permanent collection of the Smithsonian Institute National Design at the Cooper Hewitt. The calendar has won international awards for graphic design, including at AIGA Graphic Design USA and Product Design 3.

Copyright Florville Catalyst, Inc.

DESIGN
Oksana Kapranova

Game Calendar 2014

The game calendar consisted of 12 board games with each game representing one month. Each game was a module built as a cube. The games included Twister® for fingers, darts, finger soccer, checkers, and more. Each cube was stacked in a tube that could be hung on the wall. Every month the bottom cube would be removed and the next would fall down into its place.

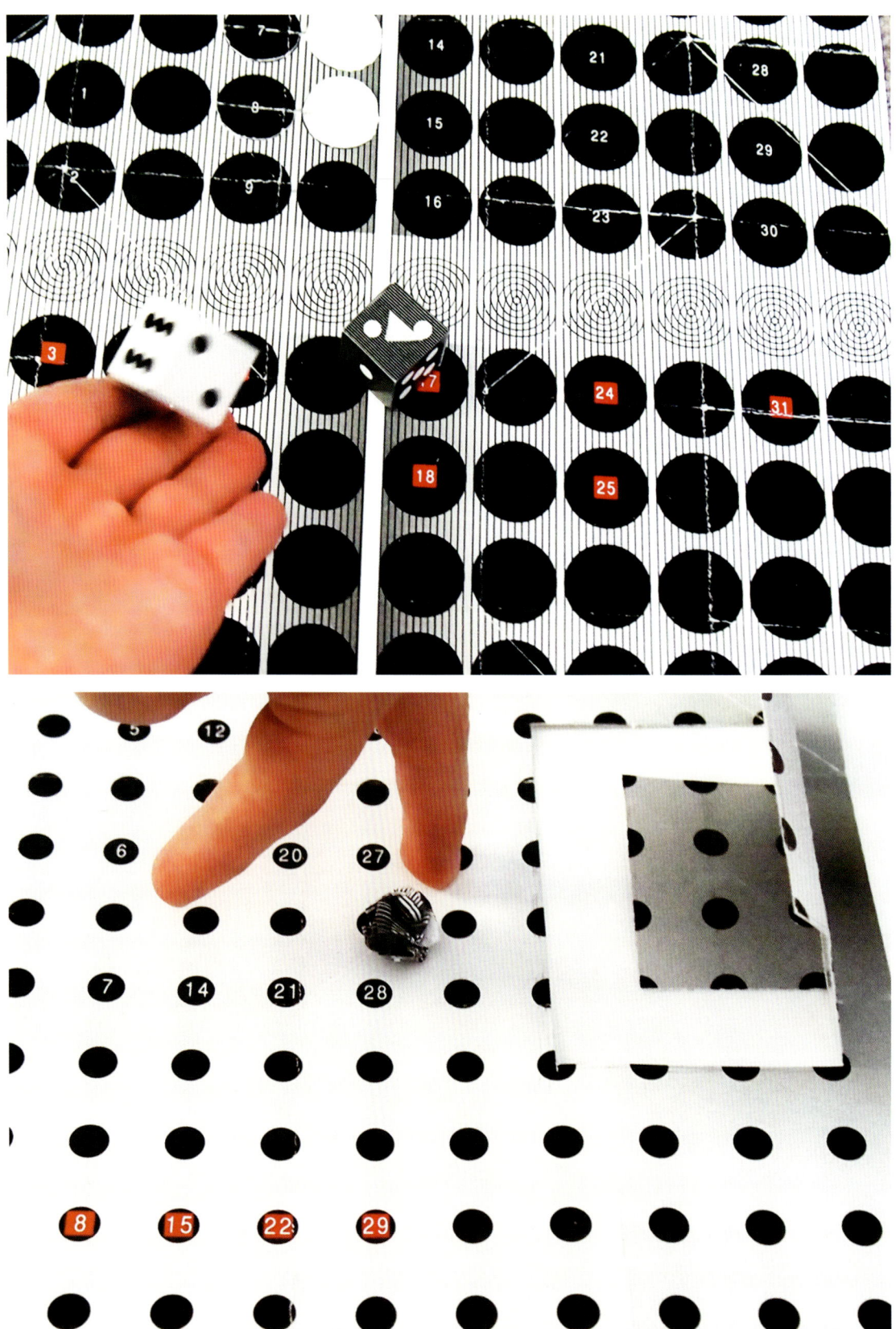

DESIGN
Maïté Chapelle

The 2012 Lovers' Calendar

Although calendars are by definition usually ephemeral, designer Maïté Chapelle wanted to create a calendar to be a sweet piece of everyday decoration that people would want to hang on their walls, and that would play with different shades, colors, and hues. Romanticism in Europe called for pulling the petals off of flowers, assigning to each a *He/She loves me a little — a lot — passionately — madly — not at all*, depending on the number of petals. This notion was featured on top of the calendar packaging, and reflected in the passage of time through the seven petals of the calendar: *Monday — Tuesday — Wednesday*, etc. The days pass faster than seasons; since they reflect the rhythm of our lives, they deserve some attention as well. A third quotation appeared in the center of the flowers, reading "*Day after day, petal after petal*," since pulling a petal each day in this romantic way evoked a feeling of jumping from one petal to the next.

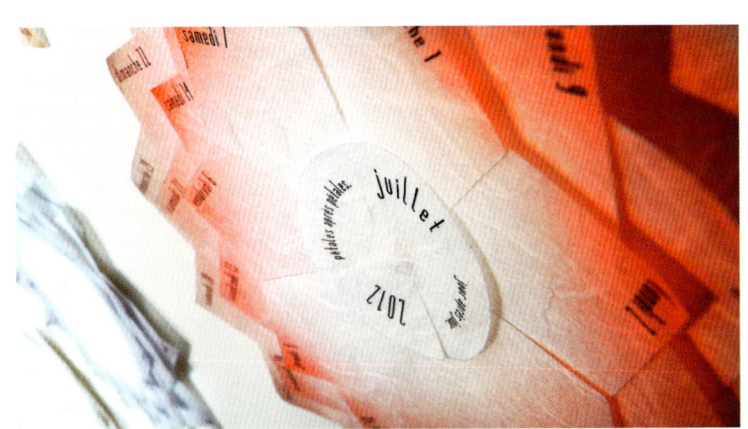

DESIGN
Vladmir Masyuk

DESIGN AGENCY
VOKAMA

Calendar

This project was based on the scheme of a dodecahedron. Designer Vladmir Masyuk decided to construct a calendar in the form of a dodecahedron using several different materials, namely wood, aluminum, and Plexiglas®. Each dodecahedron had a carton frame base. The calendars were manufactured with laser cutting and engraving, and were initially created as a New Year's gift for 2014.

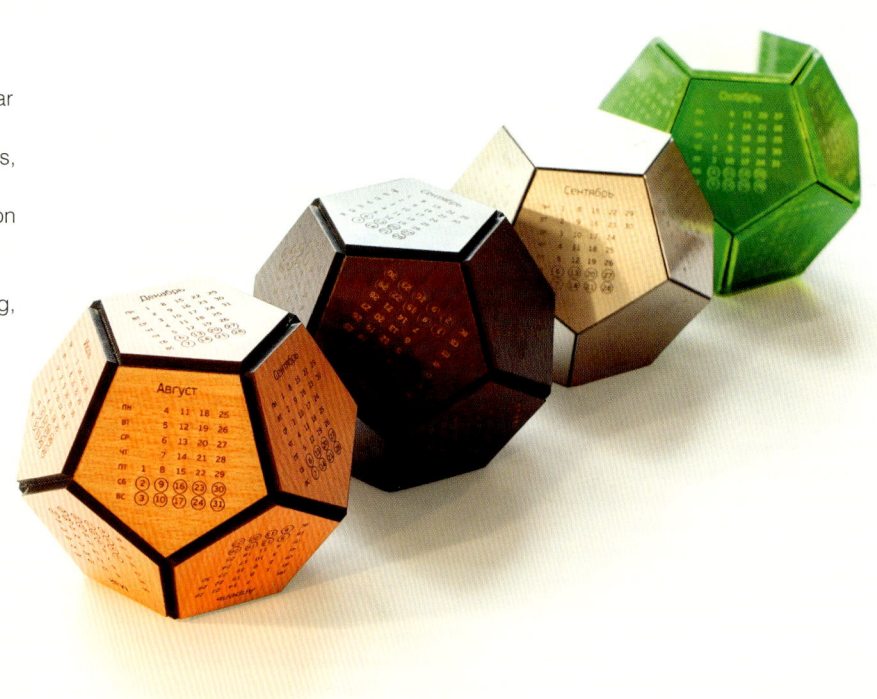

DESIGN: Vladimir Masyuk
DESIGN AGENCY: VOKAMA

Ice Sandwich Calendar

This calendar's stacking construction is reminiscent of a mini-Meccano. The current month sits on the first place, with the others visible beneath it. The modular grid used results in a 3D effect when it is viewed. To change the month, users remove the front plate and fix it at the back of the calendar. The only material used was fluorescent Plexiglas®, engraved and cut by laser.

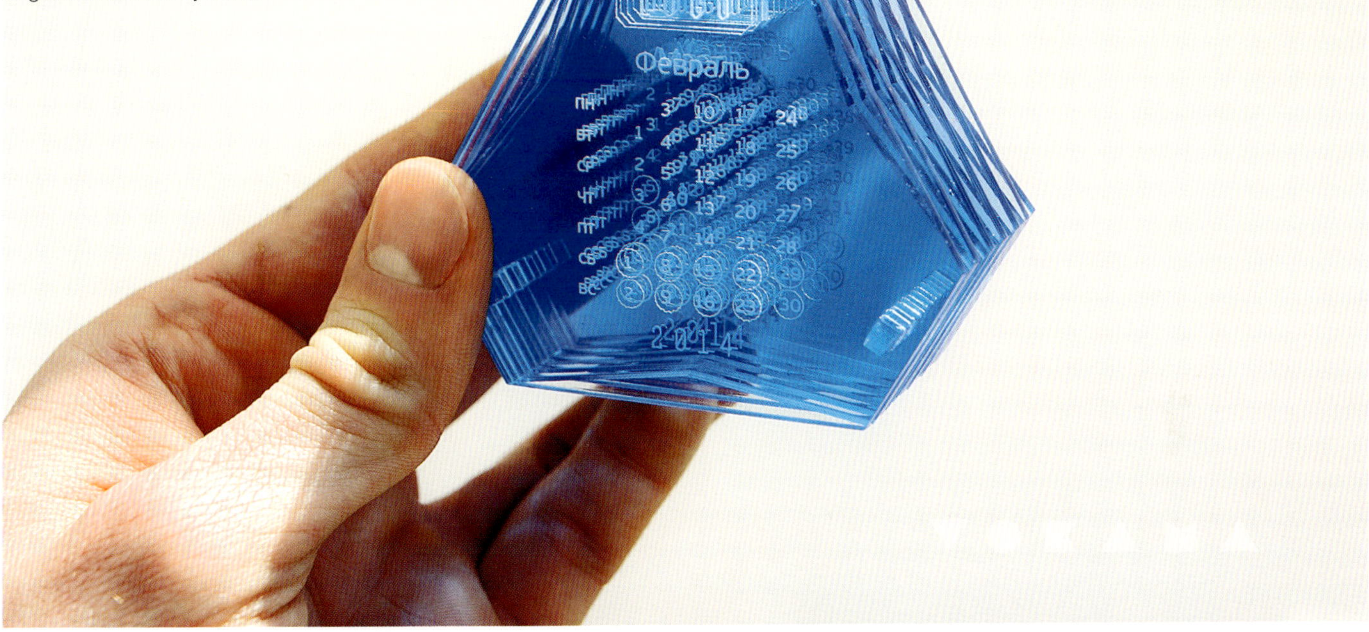

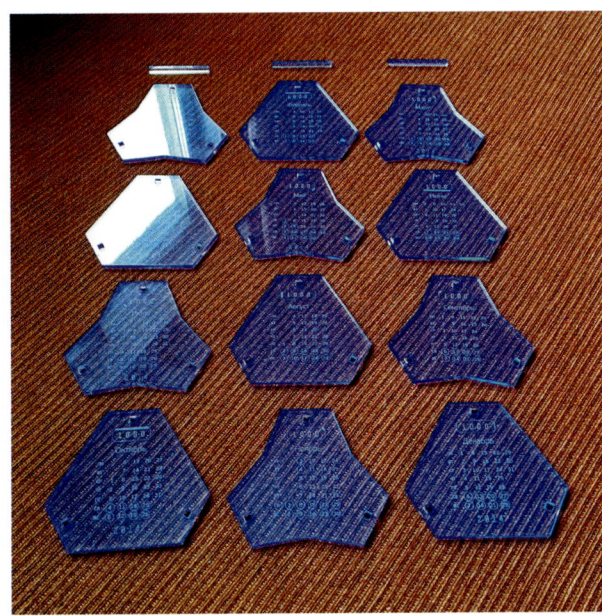

DESIGN
Janilie Fleury

Chocoaday

The design of this eco-friendly advent calendar was conceived to require the least amount of packaging materials as possible. Its compact size was meant to compete with the overpacked advent calendars that are currently on the market. The cylindrical form of Chocoaday plays on the size of the chocolate sticks inside; each day, the next chocolate is larger than the previous one.

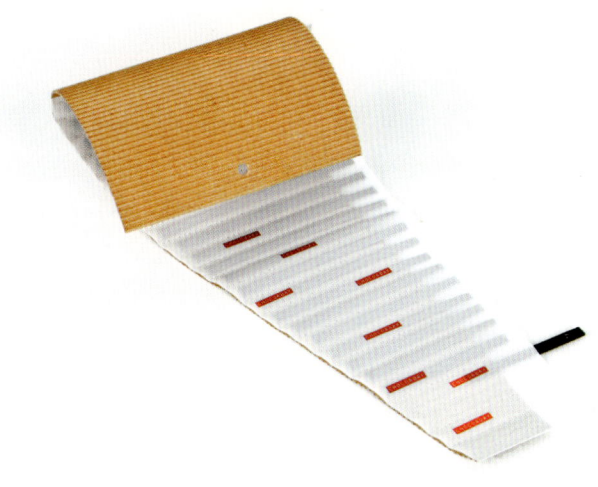

DESIGN
Sebatian Bergne

Ring Calendar

This endless wall calendar was created not just to keep people informed, but to give them the everyday satisfaction of interacting with its calm composition.

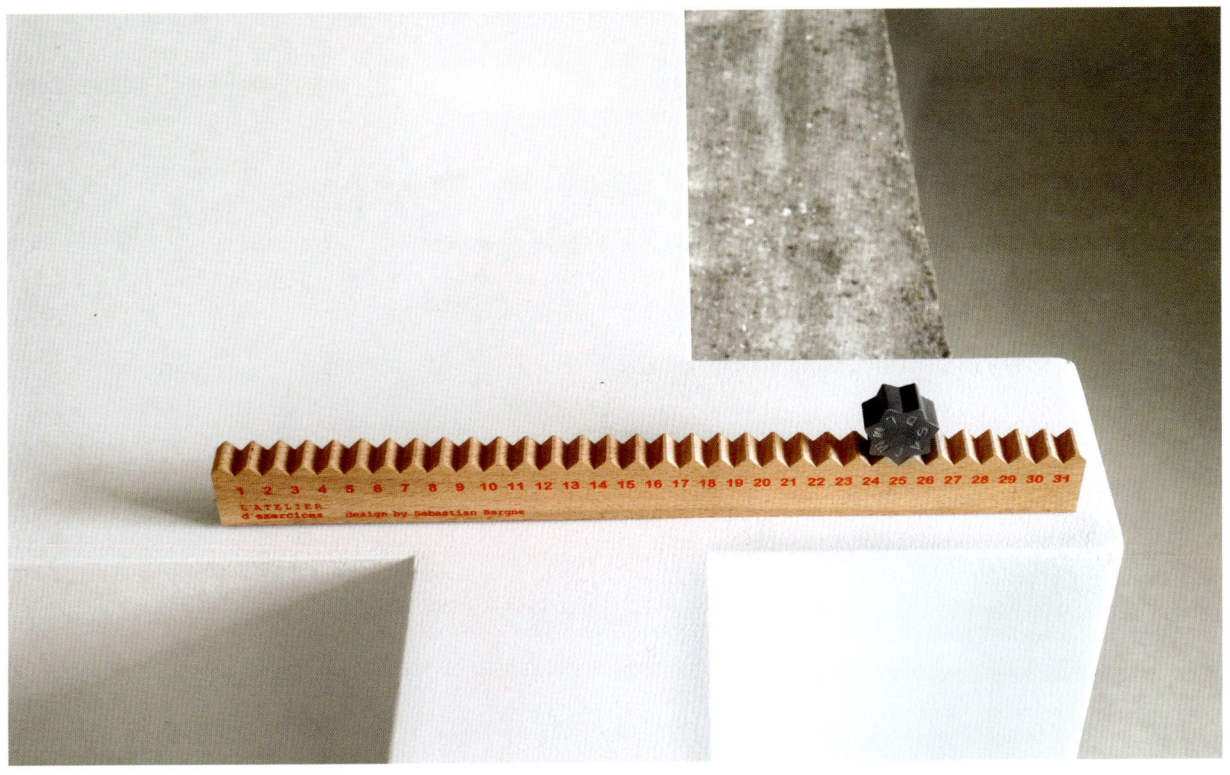

DESIGN
Alexandra Tuck

PRODUCTION
Alexandra Tuck

086

Fedrigoni 2015 Desk Calendar

Fedrigoni's Woodstock paper range was "natural in body & soul with genuine, essential colors." The brief, set by the YCN Student Awards, asked participants to design a desk calendar for Fedrigoni customers this new paper range. This calendar took the natural wood aspect literally, and based the design on a tree trunk. Each month used a different circle made of the different colors and weights of the paper range. The days of the week were etched into the wooden base, and the corresponding date in the circular paper design. The calendar reinforced the environmentally friendly nature of the paper. The calendar reinforced the environmentally friendly nature of the paper, and had a secondary use; a perforated section in the center of each month could be removed and added to a provided keyring, creating a swatch of the Woodstock range for users to keep for future reference.

DESIGN
Pattapong Mekavarakul

Right Person, Wrong Time

A series of typographic works in the theme of "Right Person, Wrong Time," inspired by the famous Thai tragic romance novel *Behind the Painting* by Sri Burapha in which the main conflict is caused by time. The designer's intention was to portray time as nonlinear through a calendar, showing it as an aspect of life that is unpredictable and illusionary. The calendar was composed of four pieces that each contained three months. To use the calendar users would place the pieces in chronological order against a wall. When a month had passed, the top piece is rotated to reveal the next month.

DESIGN
Kate Fawcett

Fedrigoni Perprtual Desk Calendar: "22 Colours, 132 Weights, 166 Days"

A perpetual desk calendar combined with a swatch book, promoting the Fedrigoni Woodstock range. Weight examples in swatch books were often limited, so this design resolved the issue by including all 132 weights available within the 22 colors of the ranges. Each paper swatch featured an illustration inspired by the names of each color, which also served to demonstrate how well ink prints on the recycled paper. The swatches could be fanned out to compare and contrast with other weights and colors.

DESIGN
Sean Anthony Murphy

PHOTOGRAPHY
Sean Anthony Murphy

092

Fedrigoni Woodstock 2015

A desk calendar for Fedrigoni, an Italian paper manufacturer, made to showcase their Woodstock paper range. The user received a hand crafted wooden box containing the calendar and a related wall calendar. Throughout the year the user's classic Italian masterpiece started to take shape.

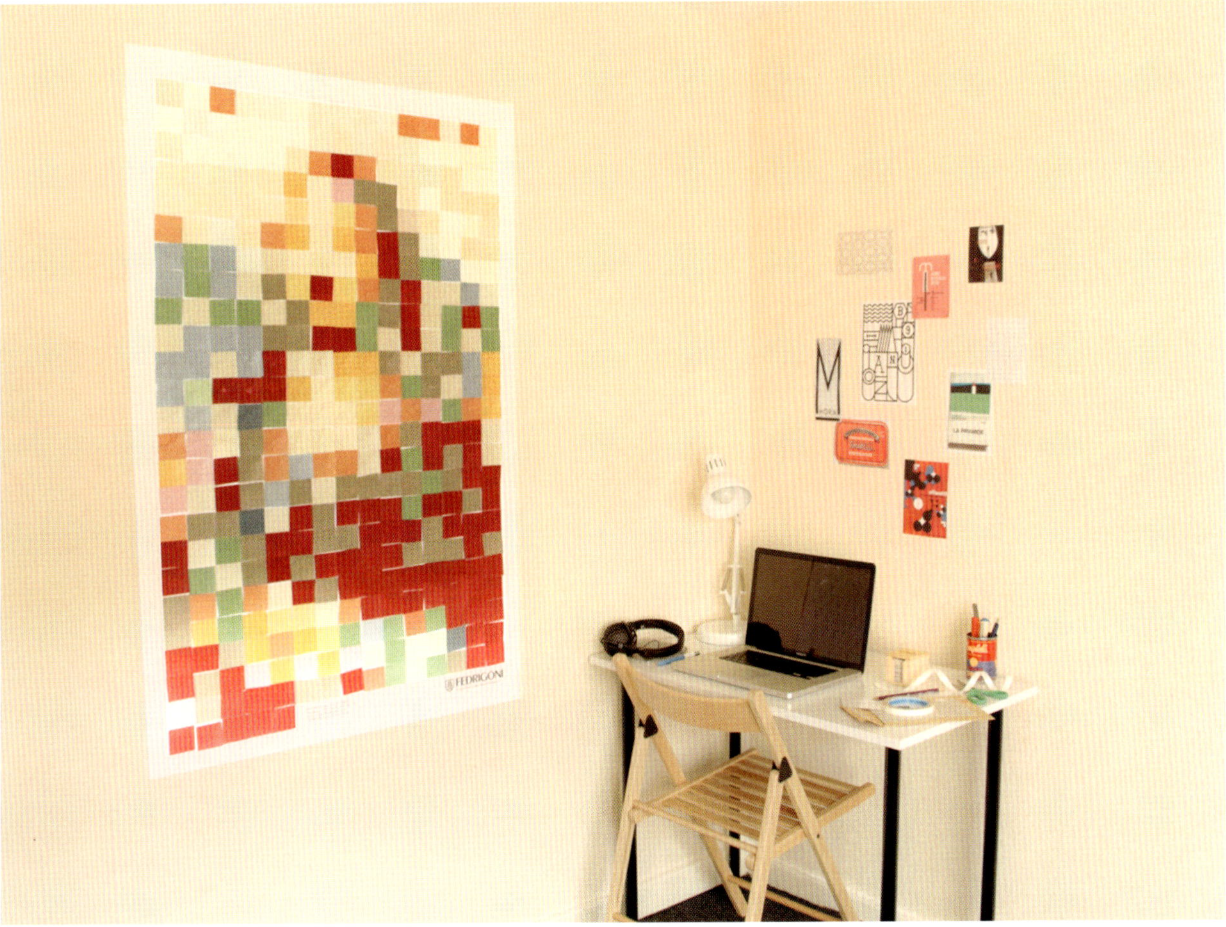

DESIGN
Enrico Salis

Taylor Made Time

This endless calendar features an hourglass crossed by two sliders of 12 and 31 cm, that respectively indicates the months and days of the year. Each calendar came packaged in a wooden container, made from the negative part of the laser cut production process. This container could also be reused as a tray or table center. The hourglass is easily and quickly mounted on a wall using double-sided adhesive tape.

DESIGN
Ivana Vucic

DESIGN AGENCY
Hamper Studio / Laboratorium

Everlasting Adhesive Calendar

A planner, a post-it, a sticker, or just regular tape. The Everlasting Adhesive Calendar was limited only by its own length. By combining two rolls of different width (one for dates, one for days of the week) the user could create any month of any calendar year.

GRAPHIC DESIGN
Hakan Aylan

ART DIRECTION
Hakan Aylan

ILLUSTRATION
Hakan Aylan & Hande Aylan

Zivaaane Filtertips Calendar

The Zivaane Filtertips Calendar was born from the search for a gift for a friend. The calendar was designed with twelve pages from January to December. Each page had perforated pieces for each day and month that could be removed and rolled into filter tips. The illustrations and typography were different on every page, so people could see different pictures just by turning the pieces.

DESIGN
Iconick

Haglöfs Interactive Calendar

This was a concertina calendar for Haglöfs | Outstanding Outdoor Equipment. It represented the life of an outdoor enthusiast. The square pages were fully foldable and each page contained inspiring quotes for that exact month. Every month contained exciting events and things to do, so a powerful calendar was necessary for every person. The quotes were Dutch but also translated to English. "You won't achieve if you don't begin."

JANUARY
"You won't achieve anything if you don't start."

MO	TU	WE	TH	FR	SA	SU
			1	2	3	4
5	6	7	8	9	10	11
12	13	14	15	16	17	18
19	20	21	22	23	24	25
26	27	28	29	30	31	

▸ new year's day

▸ alternatieve elfstedentocht weissensee

01

FEBRUARY
"Those who told you that you wouldn't make it were totally wrong."

MO	TU	WE	TH	FR	SA	SU
						1
2	3	4	5	6	7	8
9	10	11	12	13	14	15
16	17	18	19	20	21	22
23	24	25	26	27	28	

▸ kilimanjaro-man

▸ arctic weekend

02

APRIL
"Sometimes you'll get cold feet. Just be glad that you're not freezing."

MO	TU	WE	TH	FR	SA	SU
		1*	2	3	4*	5
6	7	8	9	10	11	12
13	14	15	16	17	18	19
20	21	22	23	24	25	26
27	28	29	30			

▸ scandinavian winter tour * 1 until 31

▸ start polar race

▸ fjällfest * 1 until 5

▸ valborgsmässoafton

04

JUNE
"You'll have to deal with rainfall to behold the sun in full glory after the storm."

MO	TU	WE	TH	FR	SA	SU
1	2	3	4	5	6	7
8	9	10	11	12	13	14
15	16	17	18	19	20	21
22	23	24	25	26	27	28
29	30					

▸ midsommarafton

06

AUGUST
"Be the person who accepted rain and didn't choose for shelter."

MO	TU	WE	TH	FR	SA	SU
					1	2
3	4	5	6	7	8	9
10	11	12	13	14	15	16
17	18	19	20	21	22	23
24	25	26	27	28	29	30
31						

▸ björkliden arctic mountain marathon

08

DECEMBER
"Be the person you want to be."

MO	TU	WE	TH	FR	SA	SU
	1	2	3	4	5	6
7	8	9	10	11	12	13
14	15	16	17	18	19	20
21	22	23	24	25	26	27
28	29	30	31			

▸ scandinavian winter tour

12

DESIGN
Arushi Khandelwal

MENTOR
Ms. Kanupriya Taneja

Calendar Design

This calendar doubled as a furniture design. Its conceptualization and presentation were concerned with understanding the most important aspect of calendar design, and with the ability to hold a viewer's interest for a long time. With these ideas in mind, and with the goal of making a calendar with an aesthetically pleasing and functional design, design student Arushi Khandelwal designed a desktop calendar that resembled the shape of a center table. The table was fully functional, and objects could be kept on the tabletop. The connection between calendar and furniture was the thread that made it acceptable to customers. The calendar could be given as a token of appreciation to customers, both those who return multiple times or those who have purchased the furniture only once.

DESIGN
Lee Jaegoo

2014 Typeface Calendar for Holiday

This calendar combined the concept of the anticipation of a holiday with a neat and clean aesthetic ideal for everyday life.

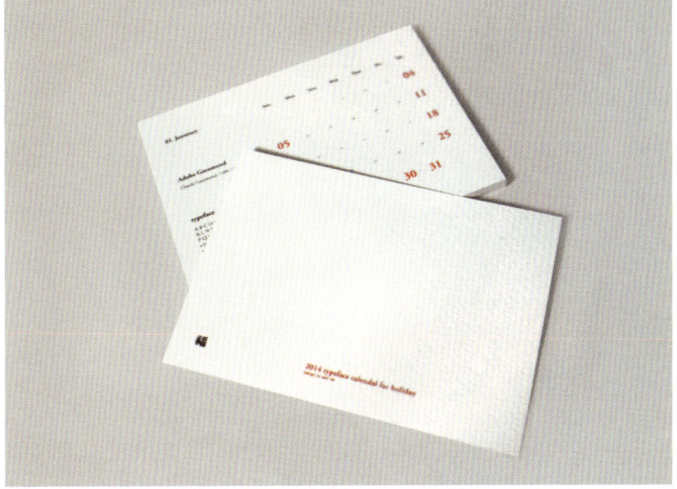

DESIGN
Kostantia Manthou

PRINTING
Legno

Fragile Pocket Calendar

Fragile Pocket Calendar was a tiny foldable and portable calendar meant only for the important stuff. In a world of digital planners, organizers, and diaries being constantly synced with every aspect of life, it's important to keep certain events in an analog format as a reminder of an older era, or simply as a form of expressing oneself analogically. The main material for the calendar was a lightweight paper that increased the feeling of fragility as well as the importance of protecting the calendar along with its cherished contents.

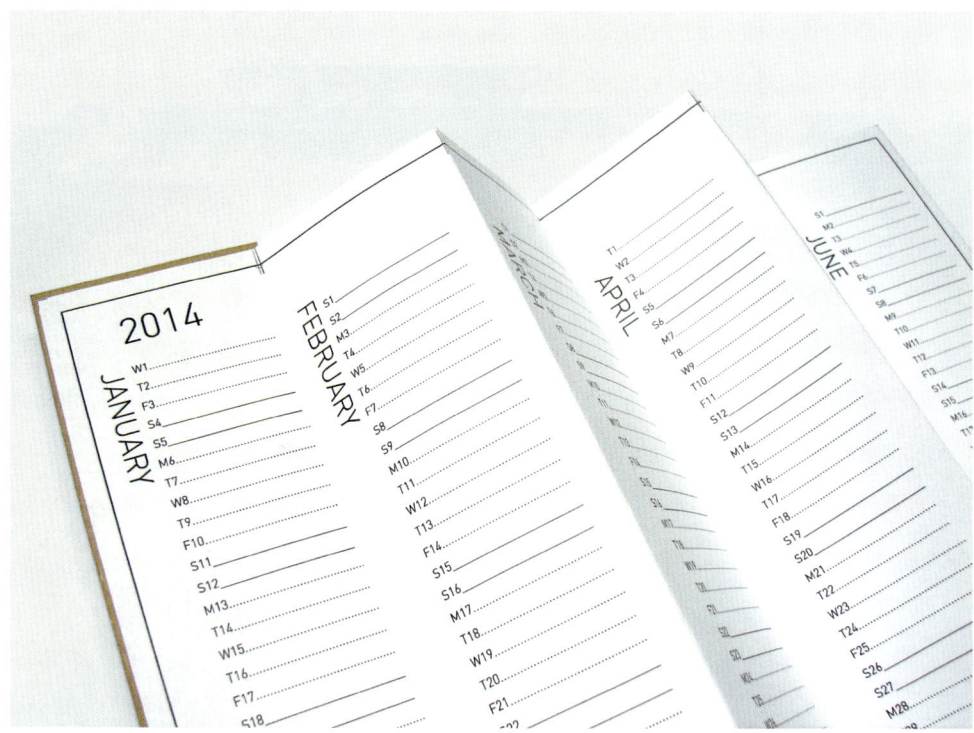

DESIGN
Vassiliki Kostoglou

ILLUSTRATION
Vassiliki Kostoglou

Bar Calendar

This was a pocket-size calendar for everyday notes. The folding concept grew from a formalist approach to the project; the goal was for the piece to give the impression of being a small abstract sculpture when it was placed on someone's desk, rather than a common calendar. The design was based on the way a sheet of paper folds in order to best save space. At the same time, depending on the way it was folded the calender could be used to depict a single month, two months simultaneously, or any other combination.

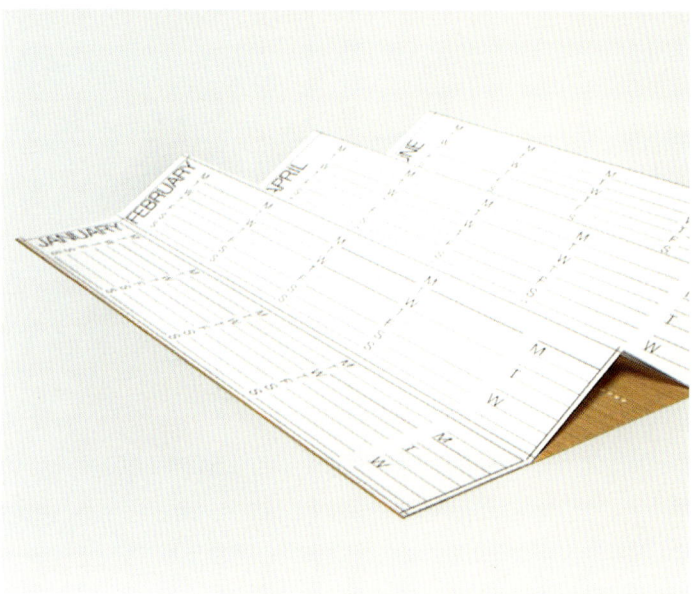

111

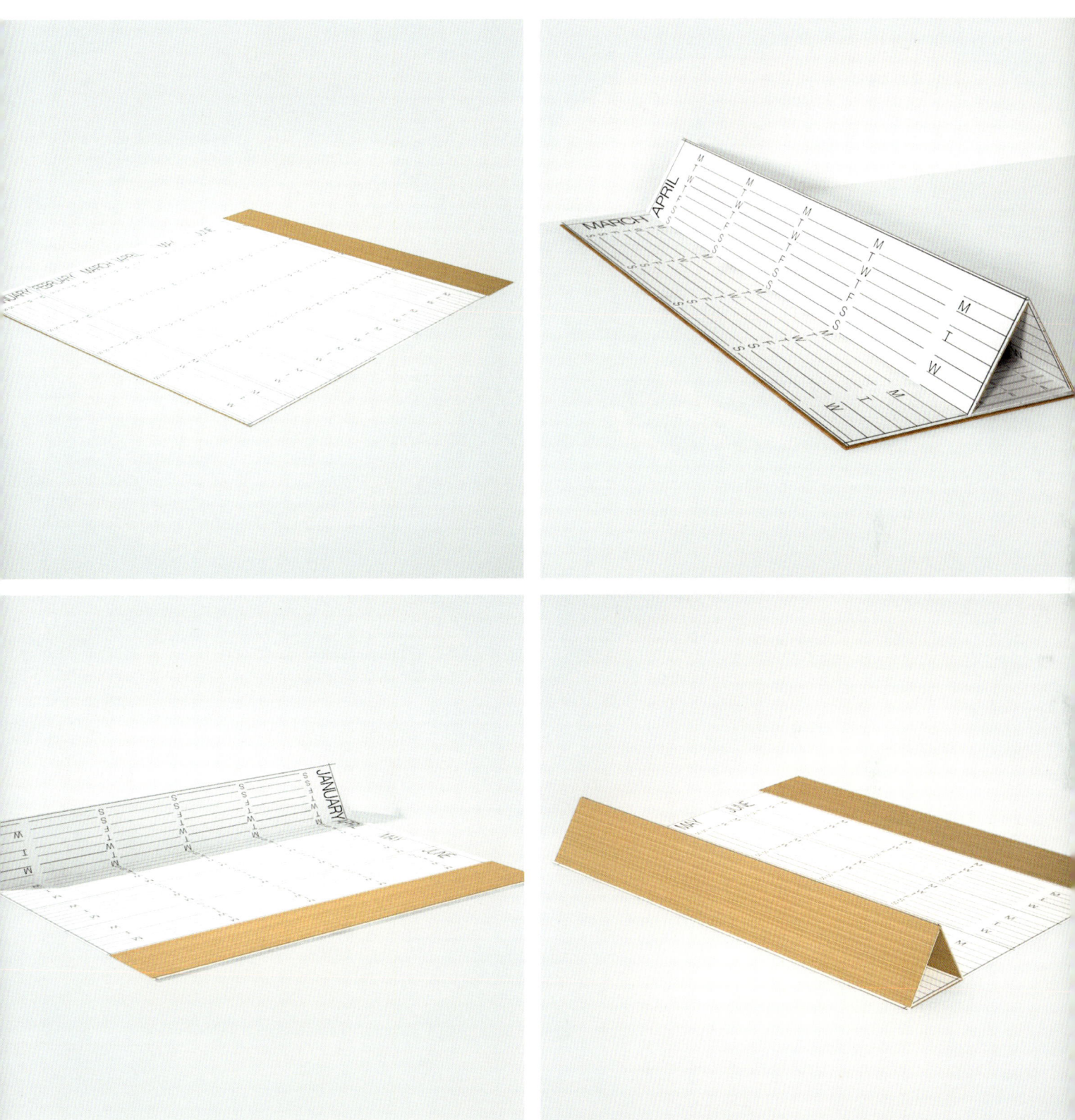

DESIGN AGENCY
Visitors

Twelve Horses 2014

2014 was the Year of the Horse according to Chinese zodiac. Twelve Horses 2014 was a self-promotion poster calendar that showcased twelve different horses in Chinese context. Each typography design was designed with its own unique symbolic characteristic and each of them represented a specific month of the year. The twelve horses draw people closer to observe and learn through the journey of cultural exploration and experience.

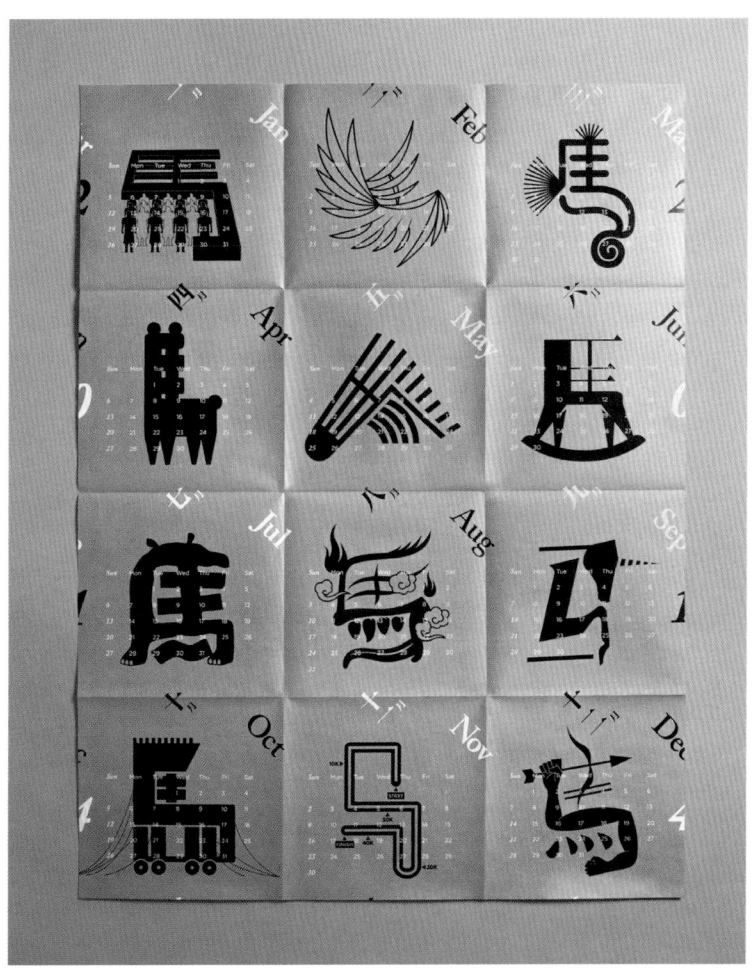
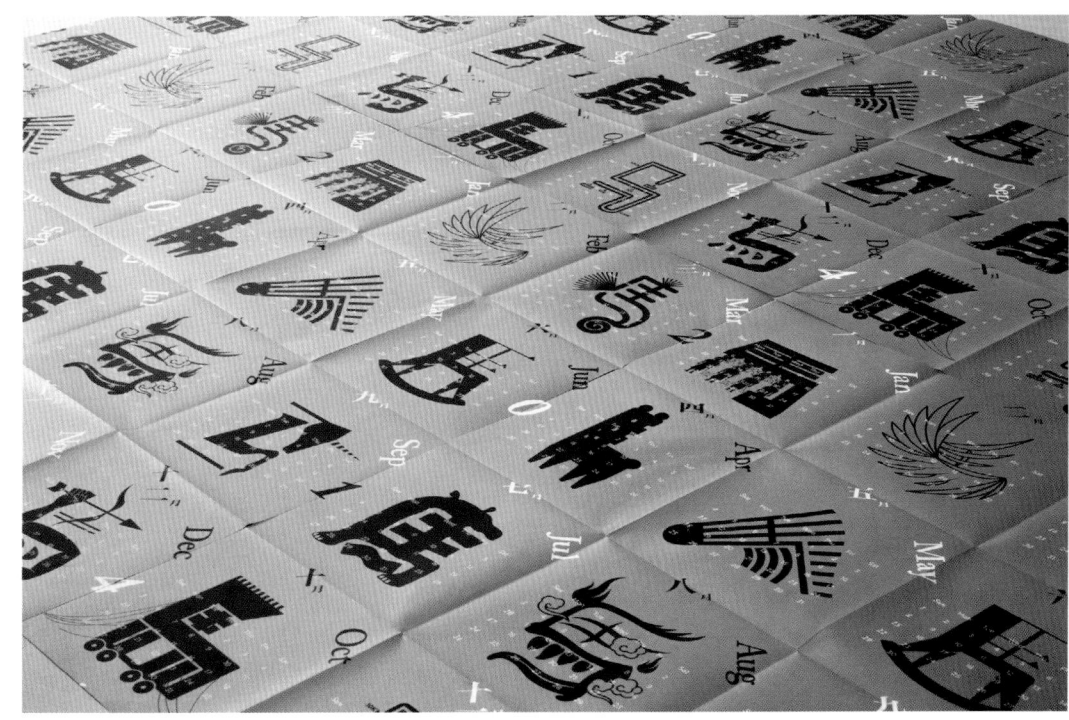

CONCEPT & DESIGN
Agnė Dautartaitė-Krutulė.

PHOTOGRAPHY
Modestas Ežerskis.

ARTWORKS
Severija Inčirauskaitė-Kriaunevičienė

Art Catalog for Severija Inčirauskaitė – Kriaunevičienė

The main idea behind this calendar was to connect the works of the artist (the stitched art objects) and the characteristics of old-fashioned garden calenders together as one. The work was made to be functional while simultaneously serving as an art catalog. A poster with seasonal themes represented each month, and every day was a fragment of the whole poster. The calendar had every component of a book (such as text, illustration, meter, a colophon, and even pagination), and all of the technological processes and specifications of a daily gardener's calendar.

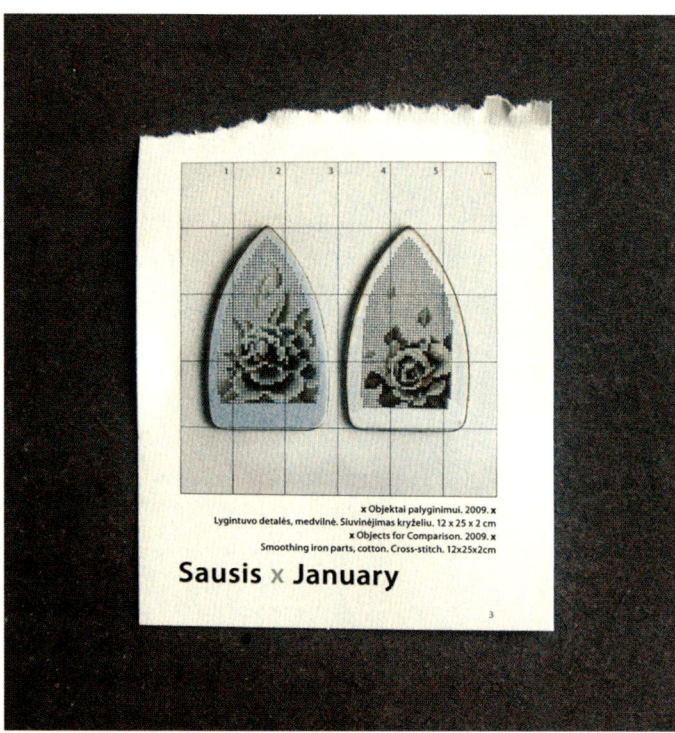

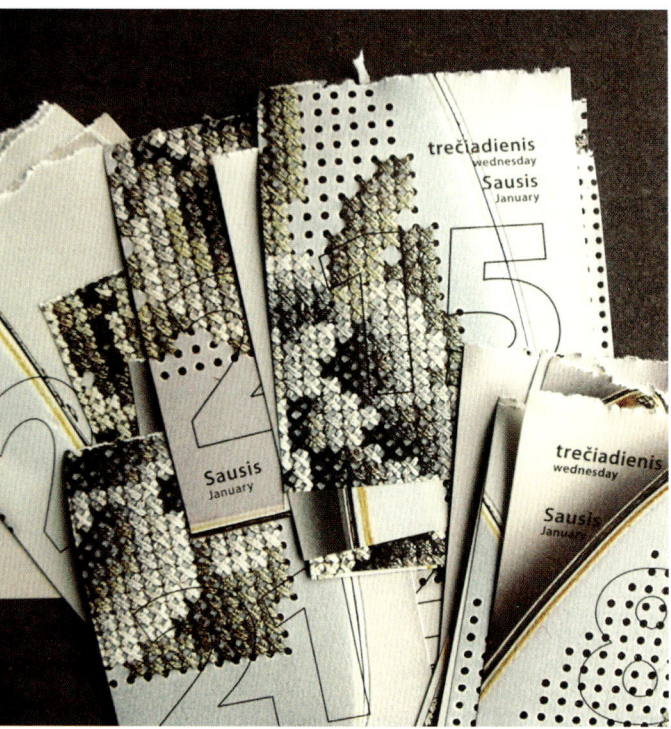

CALENDAR 2014

Calendar

This was a Norwegian calendar which could be transformed into greeting cards. One side of the calendar showed the month, the dates, and a graphical decorative element. The elements were inspired by mandalas and were based on the Norwegian seasons and traditions. On the other side of the calendar there was a greeting card for each month which represented something special for that month. By ripping off the month and dates, the calendar could be used as a decorative card for people to give to each other on special days.

DESIGN
Mattea Stahl & Tamara Haake

Time Zone Calendar

The world is divided into 24 time zones – this calendar displays all of them on one date sheet. The user simply needs to find the time zone and adjust the current date against the colored rail to show the different times in the other parts of the world. Individual months were shown below the calendar to enable the sheet to be used through the entire year. On the back of the cover there was an overview of the time zones with their biggest cities to help people find the time of their friends and family around the globe.

DESIGN
Laura Wallbridge-Bruce

YCN Fedrigoni Calendar

This calendar, designed for the use of graphic designers, was submitted to the YCN Student Awards competition. It was designed in a concertina format to minimize the amount of space it would take up on a desk. The shape of the Fedrigoni logo was used to create a window through which the colors of the Woodstock range could be viewed. The calendar was effortlessly simple to use. Each month, a different piece of paper could be removed and revealed to the user. The months also included a list of the different weights and details of the chosen stock, allowing the calendar to also act as a stock guide for the Woodstock range. As there are 22 colors in the range, each month displayed two different stock choices. December and January were the only months that displayed one stock, which left extra room for potential text, such as "Happy New Year" or "Happy Holidays."

DESIGN
Akira Kusaka

ILLUSTRATION
Akira Kusaka

Calendar Design of 2014

This calendar was designed by freelance illustrator and graphic designer Akira Kusaka. Every illustration was one of his painted works in 2013.

DESIGN AGENCY
STUDIO NEWWORK

NEWWORK
Calendar 2014

Dates were composed as music notes, and each month played a different melody. This peaceful calendar featured 12 monthly cards (plus a cover page) with corresponding envelopes. This encouraged people to write a note and use the cards not just as a calendar, but also as message cards for birthday, anniversaries, and other special events.

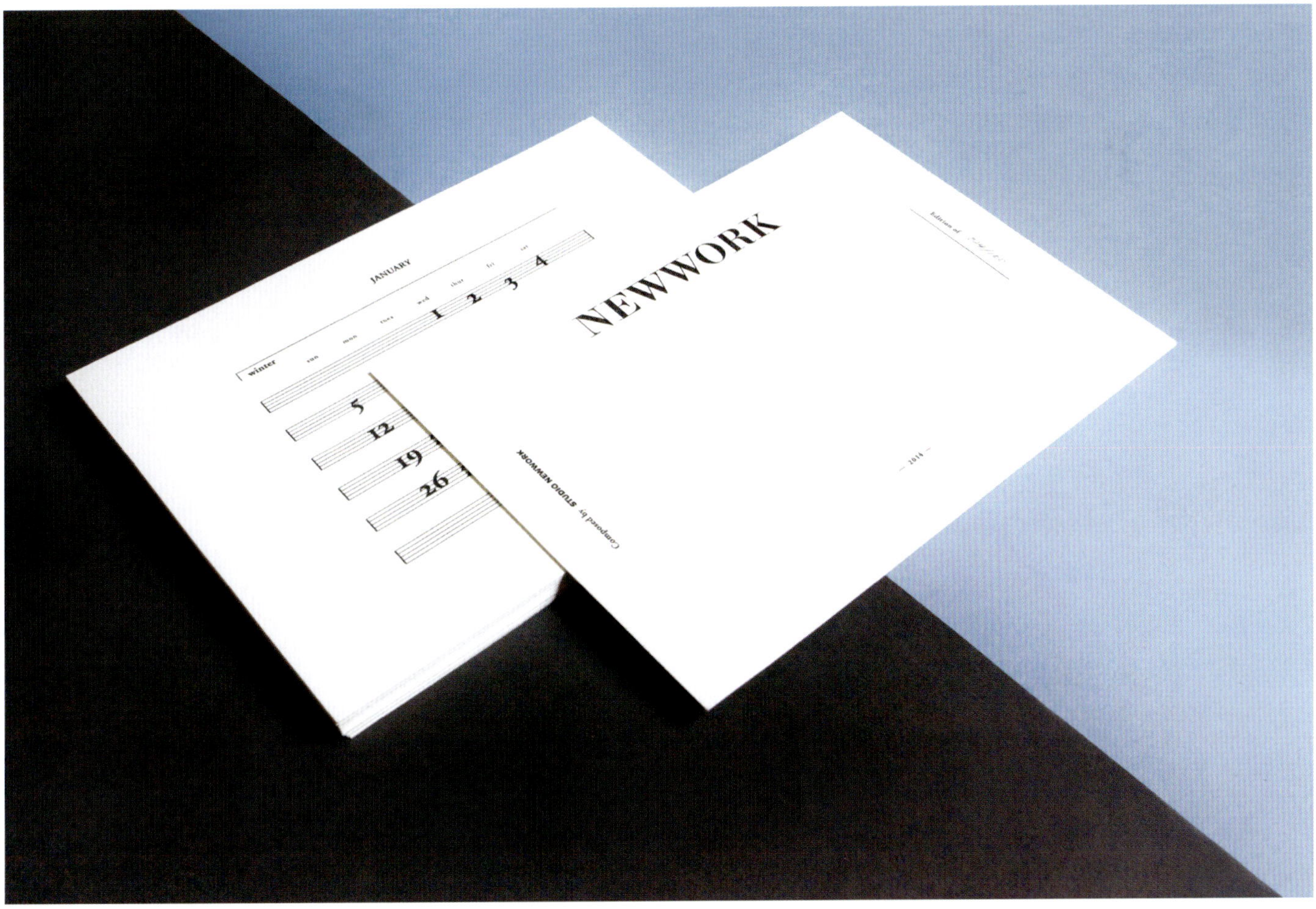

DESIGN
Éva Somogyi

Calendar-Pop-up Poem Book

This 3D poem book was using pop-up techniques, and was inspired by the twentieth-century Hungarian poet Miklós Radnóti's lyrical cycle titled "Calendar." The spatial compositions in the twelve spreads were linked to the main theme – the changes in nature with the seasons of the year. The small paper creations reflected the atmosphere and cyclical nature of the seasons in a clear but lyrical and sensitive way, just as the poems did. The designer consciously avoided the use of color in every aspect but the typography, allowing incidental light, shadow, and contrast to create a smooth harmony of natural colors.

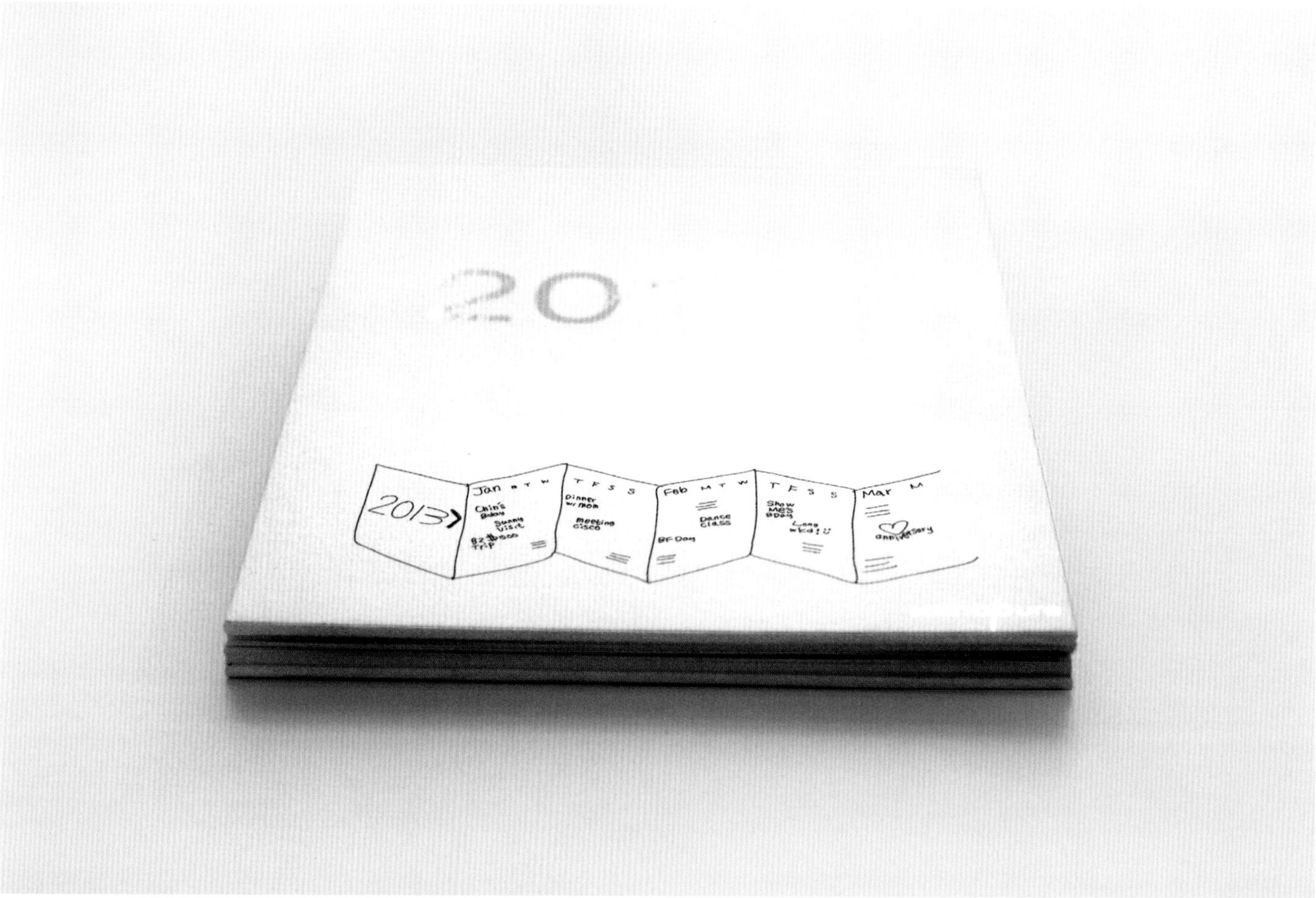

DESIGN
Sasha Tseng

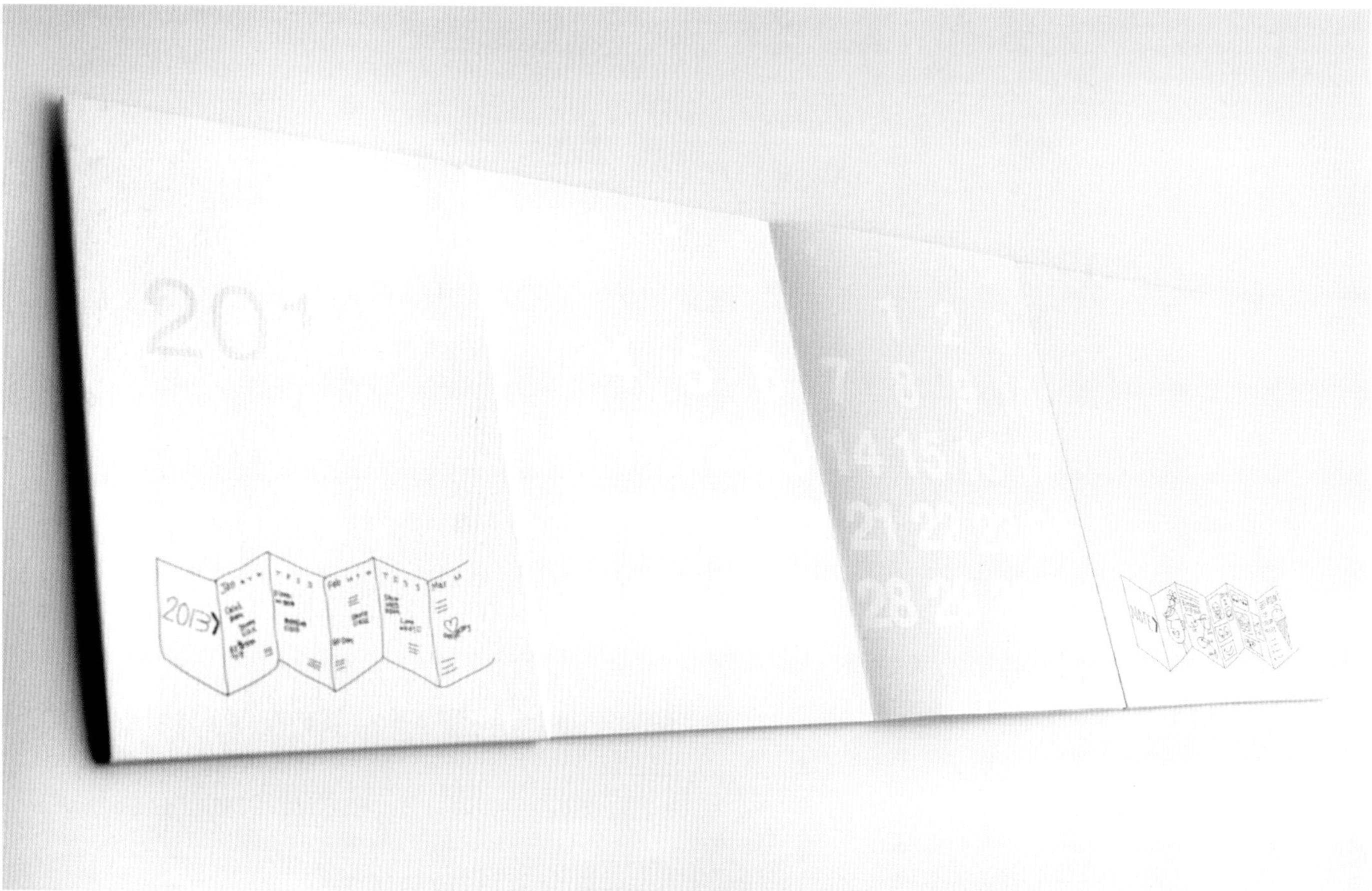

Invisible Calendar

The Invisible Calendar was designed to encourage creative thinking. The dates on the calendar were printed with clear ink, resulting in it looking like a piece of plain paper; however, the important dates and events people wrote on the calendar would show crystal clear, since all of the unimportant extra information was "invisible." The Invisible Calendar could be opened to show all 12 months at once and gave users a new perspective by showing them the entire year on a single page. The reverse side was blank and could be used as a notepad, giving people extra room to write down daily activities or notes.

DESIGN
Isabelle Mattern

CONCEPT
Isabelle Mattern

132

Student Organizer - Time is of the Essence

The student organizer was designed with the BA Graphic Design Course at the Central Saint Martins in mind. The course's timetable revolved around each chosen three-week-project, so it was up to the students to independently manage their time throughout the weeks. The Calendar was divided into three terms of the school year, and each contained a term overview page, ten-week pages, a notes block and a legend block. While the sheets could be used individually or together, a set of customizable stamps served as a tool for visual representations of the different projects and encouraged an individual interaction with the organizer. It was a calendar that catered to its user and could be adapted to a variety of circumstances.

DESIGN AGENCY
Lo Siento

2012 Lo Siento Calendar

2012 Calendar was made by Lo Siento and was intended to be given as a gift. Each month showed a polyhedron with a different number of faces that corresponded to the number of the month.

DESIGN
Ainorwei Lin

PHOTOGRAPHY
Ainorwei Lin

Natural (2014 Calendar)

A gypsy legend said that humans were born with "color natures," meaning that everyone has different "color natures" according to the season and nature's changes when they were born. The designer used symbolic figures and colors to represent the meaning of every month on this calendar, as well as careful typographic choices in order to enhance the aesthetic value of the calendar.

DESIGN AGENCY
Studio Lin

Studio Lin x Linco 2012 Calendar

Studio Lin teamed up with their favorite NYC newspaper printer to create a 2012 calendar. Each of the 12 poster sized months features a different spot color and paper. All together, the package represented everything that Linco Printing was capable of and served as a great reference for designers looking to see actual paper and color samples.

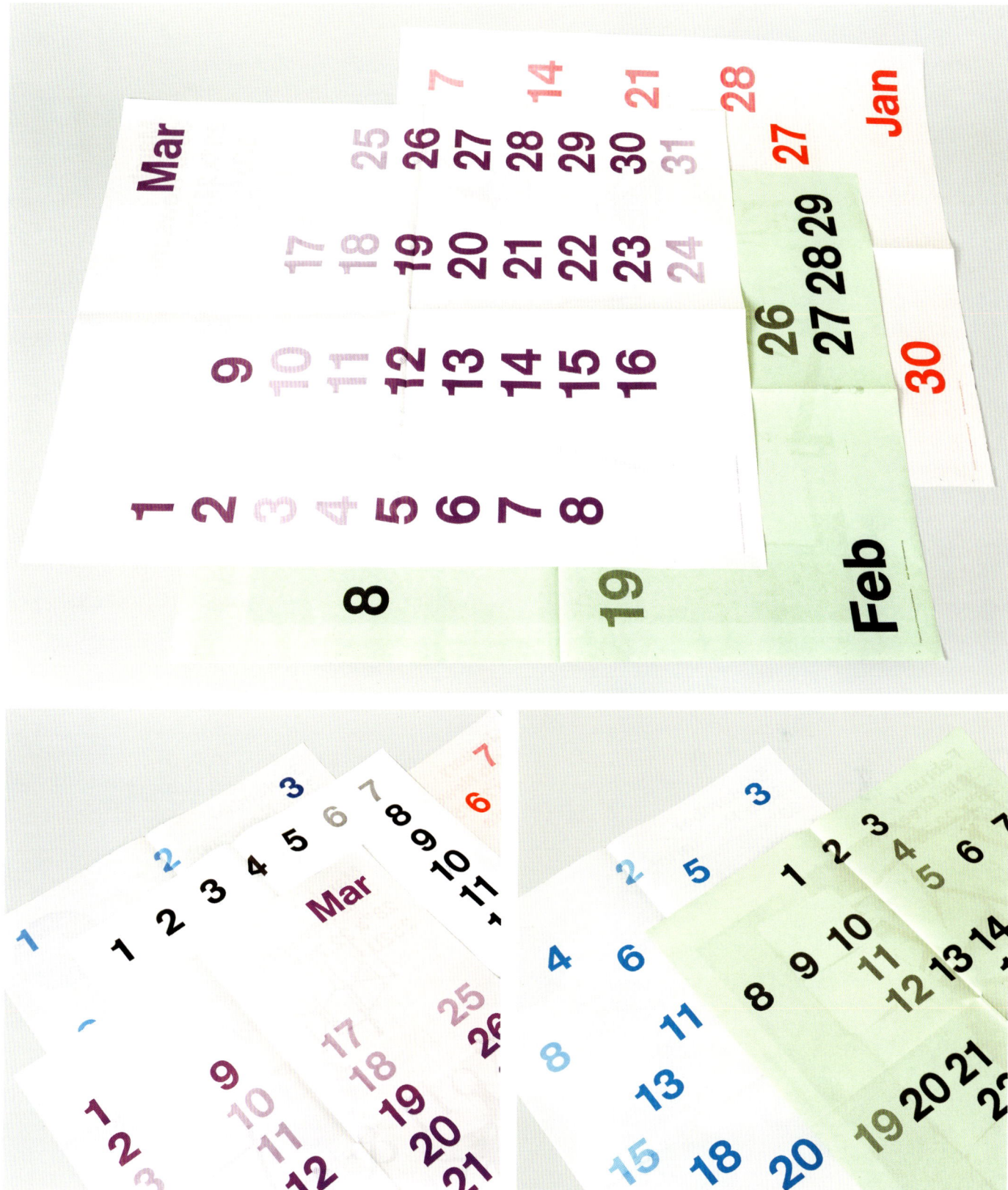

Bearded Calendar

In the spirit of the revitalized popularity of funky and outrageous facial hair, it seemed reasonable to do a project that celebrated beards. The Bearded Calendar was a weekly calendar for the year 2015 that showed the passage of time through the growth of various types of beards. There were 12 beards in total, one for every month.

DESIGN
João Araújo

DESIGN AGENCY
And Atelier

FPCEUP Calendars

Each year, the Oporto Faculty of Psychology and Educational Sciences (FPCEUP) produces a small annual planner to give students a space to organize and schedule their time. Inside there is space for notes and room for people to write down their specific schedule, and the calendar of the school year is displayed on the back cover. Every year the planner is adjusted based on past reviews from the school. The agenda's cover is also redesigned yearly, with a focus on maintaining its typographic identity and clarity.

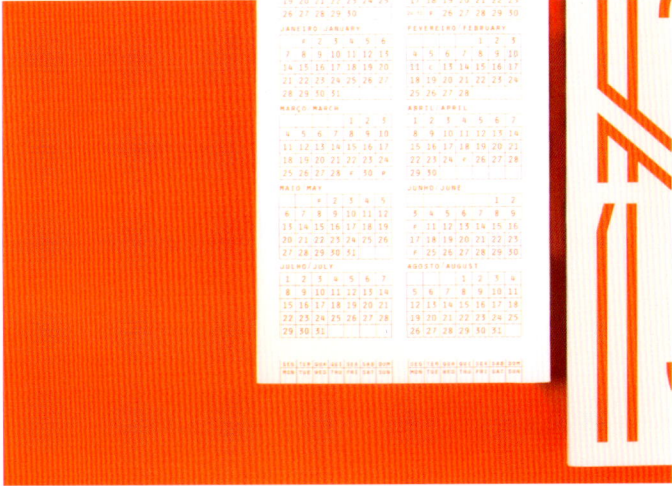

DESIGN
Adrian Meseck

CONCEPT
Adrian Meseck

Pocket Planner 2013

This pocket planner was made for people who appreciate handwriting, such as creatives, writers, or basically anyone who needs to take notes or sketch their ideas on a daily basis.

DESIGN
Jodie-Ann Langley

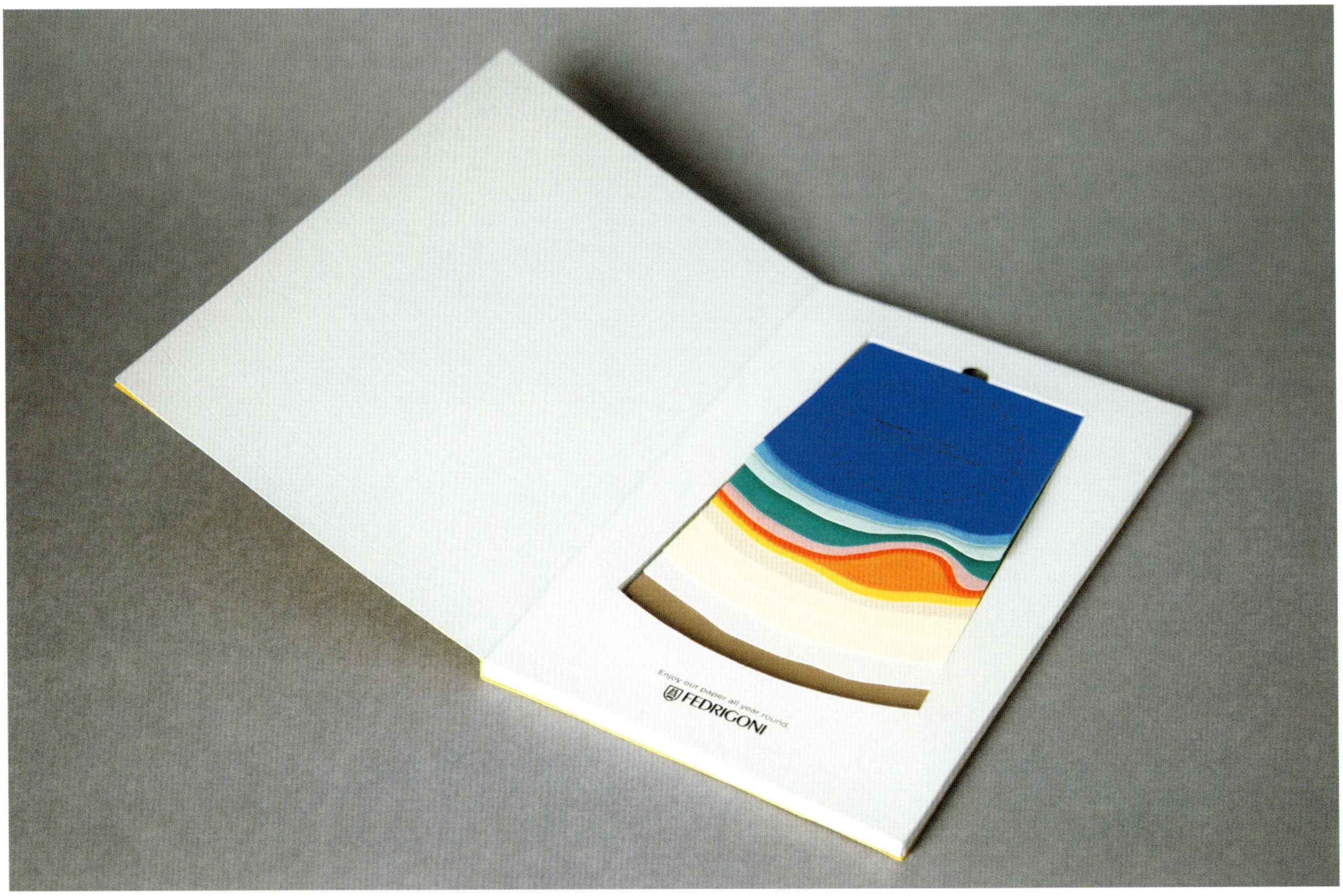

146

YCN Fedrigoni Competition Brief 2014

Woodstock was a unique paper range made from 80% recycled pre-consumer waste and 20% FSC certified Virgin fibre. The desk calendar needed to be functional and visually pleasing, whilst promoting this uncoated pulp collection of colored papers. To promote the naturalness of the Woodstock range, the 2015 Fedrigoni desk calendar took inspiration from where it originated from, the tree. The design was beautifully simplistic so as not to steal attention from the paper range to satisfy the designers who would receive the calendar.

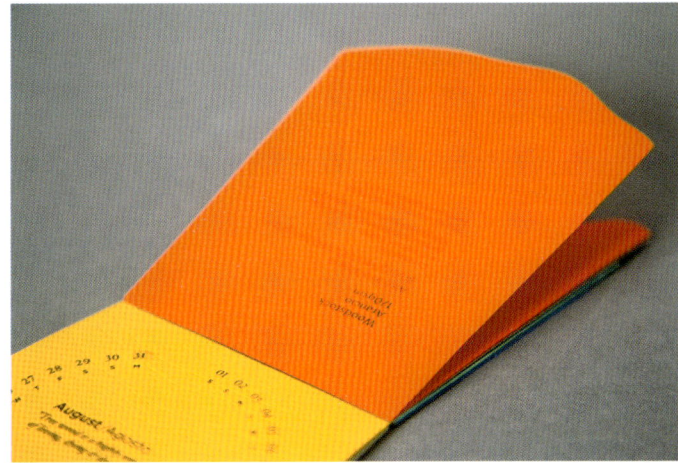

DESIGN
Calvin Tan, Dennis Koay, Tan Say Fin

Gong Xi Fa Cai

Malaysia is one of the most multicultural countries in the world, where people celebrate their traditional festivals together without worrying about race. In Malaysia, locals have their own unique way of celebrating Chinese New Year, showcased in this calendar and booklet. During Chinese New Year the most common thing said is "Gong xi fa cai" -- literally, "congratulations on getting more wealth." The humorous reply to this is "hong bao na lai," meaning "give me a red packet," referring to the traditional way of gifting money on Chinese New Year.

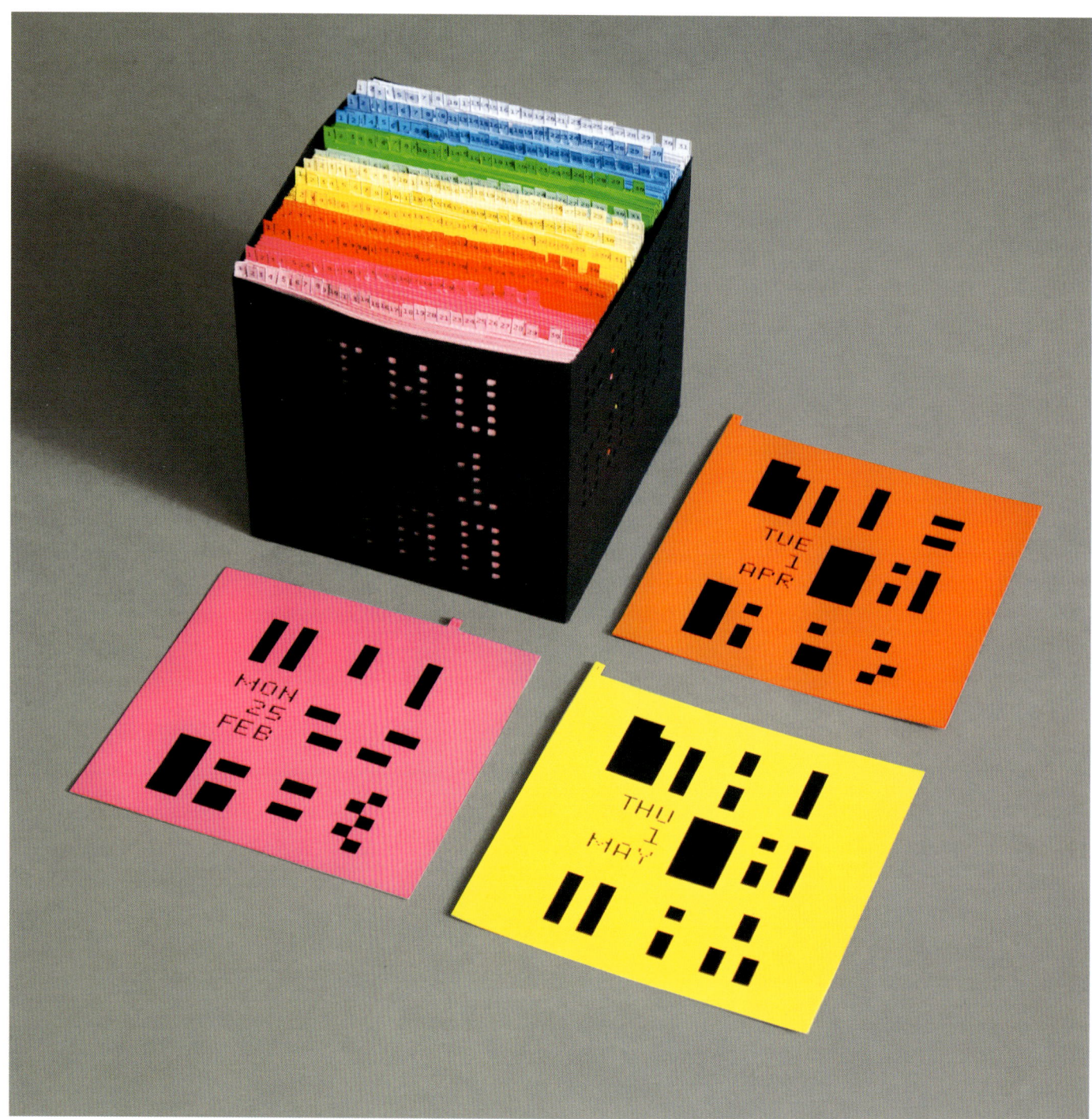

2015 Fedrigoni Calendar

This project was a response to the YCN Student Awards, the desired outcome of which was a 2015 calendar to promote Fedrigoni's Woodstock range. The daily view calendar worked on a system where each card contained cryptic rectangles which revealed the date when placed inside a matrix of squares on the face of the cubic container. Each day the user could pull out the date that had passed and move it to the back to display the next date. Significant dates, such as Christmas or New Year's Day, were displayed on the back of the corresponding cards. This feature would work especially well if used in an open-plan office.

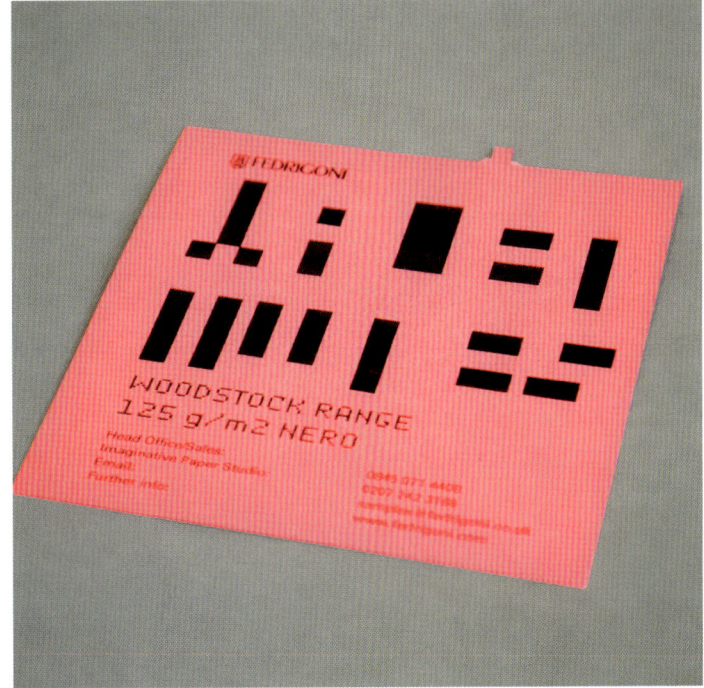

DESIGN
Emilia Emigo

Calendar Planetarium

This calendar was inspired by our solar system. Each page showed a single element of it without presenting any of them separately, and catered to the client's expectation of a modern and dynamic design. An additional advantage of the design was that it allowed for reduced printing costs compared to a traditional wall calendar.

DESIGN AGENCY
Vasava

PRODUCTION
Leicrom and Plan B

Vasava Calendar

Twaddle. Piffle. Nonsense. Whimsy. 365 silly things together in a collection of irrelevant data that eveyone surely knew nothing about nor need to! Vasava compiled and illustrated them to accompany people throughout 2014. With the start of the new year, people had before them a blank canvas on which to paint their hopes and dreams. This calendar encouraged them to do something crazy, to fall in love, to laugh and enjoy each day to the fullest, because each day was unique and they would only get to live it once. In truth, there are only two days that are no use to people: yesterday and tomorrow. Everything that really matters has to be done today!

DESIGN
Walvis & Mosmans

DESIGN AGENCY
Walvis & Mosmans

Ando Calendar – 'The Twelve of '13'

The Ando Calendar was an annual gift from the The Hague-based printer Ando to its clients. Design Agency Walvis & Mosmans was in charge of the design and concept, and their final calendar showed the virtues of Ando's printing, binding, and design like none other. All 2000 copies were hand bound to create a unique piece of craftsmanship that was surprising in many different ways. Containing twelve separate sections, the book emphasized the passing of the year by giving each month its own pattern and color scheme.

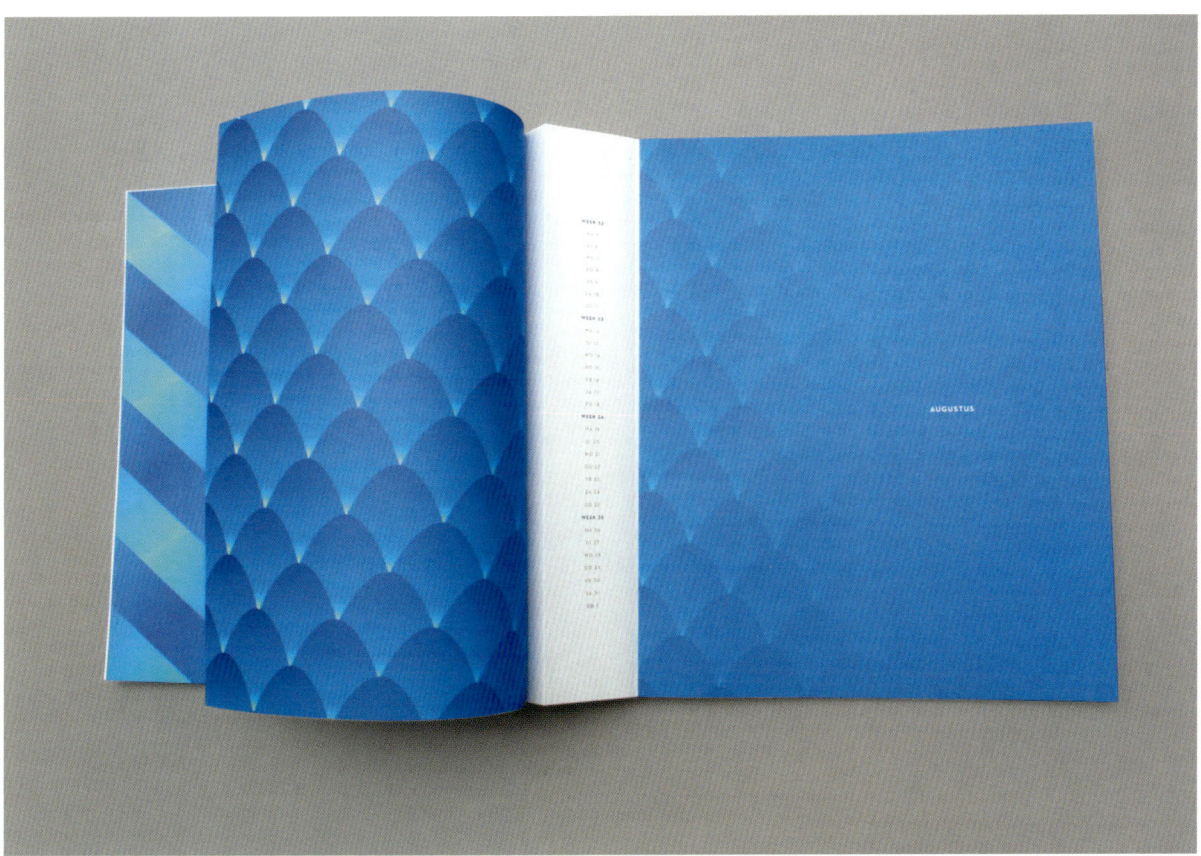

DESIGN	CONCEPT	PUBLISHER
Peter von Freyhold	Peter von Freyhold	Verlag Hermann Schmidt Mainz

C|M|Y|K Color Matching Calendar

This calendar provided a daily inspiration for color lovers. Each day a color stripe could be torn off and new color combinations came up. Printed on both coated and uncoated paper, the stripes could be collected to create color matching fans with the use of a bookbinder screw, which was integrated in the head of the calendar. The exact C|M|Y|K data were printed on every stripe. The calendar contained 371 unique color stripes, and was printed on 210 g/m² two sided chromo cardboard.

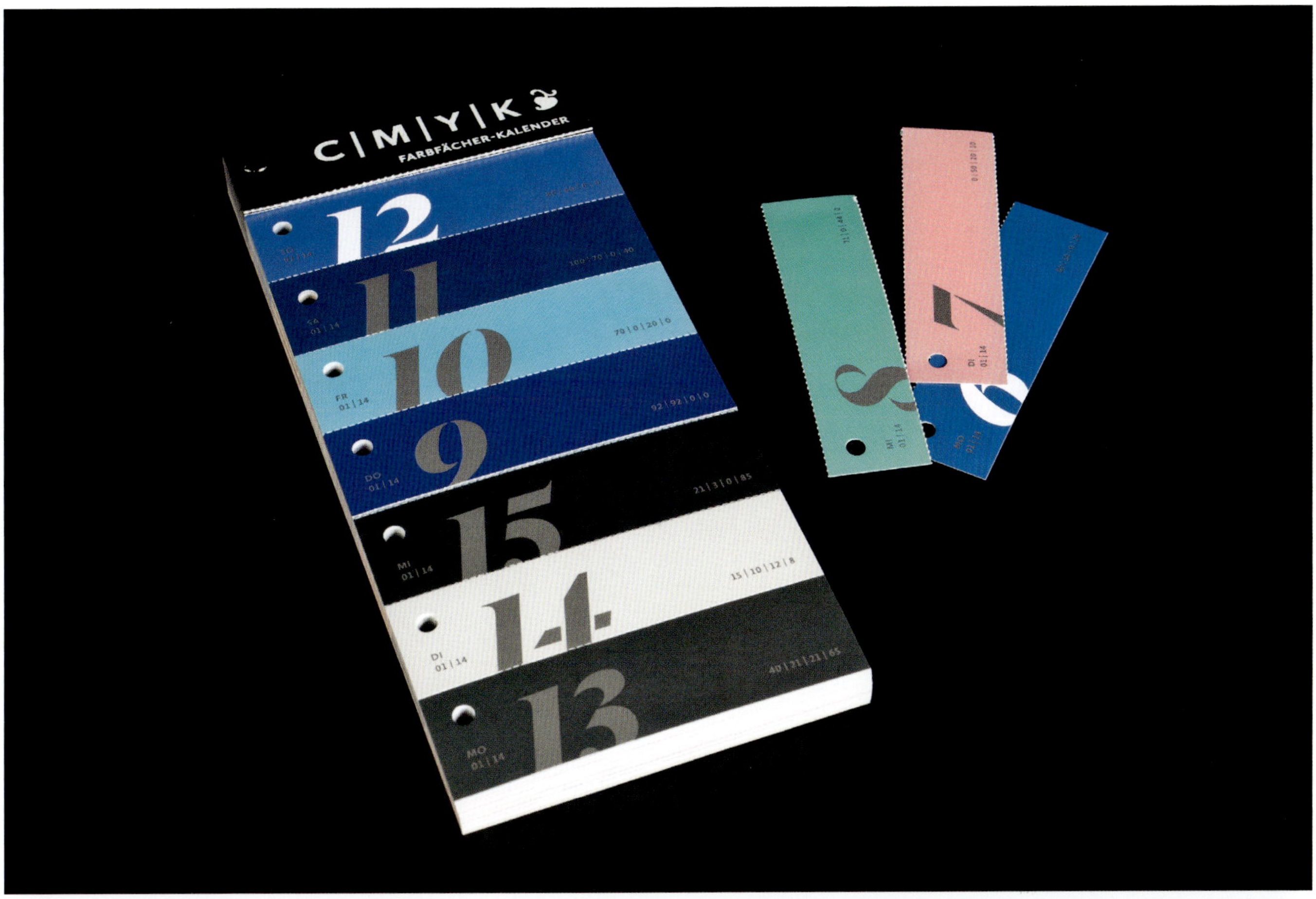

159

2015 Fedrigoni Paper Desk Calendar

This calendar was designed to be an aesthetic as well as a functional piece. Rotating the calendar gave the user key dates as well as information on the paper type used to construct that particular month. The idea was that once a month was finished, a perforated section of the card could be torn away to leave the user a swatch of the paper for future reference and a new color and paper type would take its place. As an added bonus for the user, the center prism opened up to reveal branded Fedrigoni pencils.

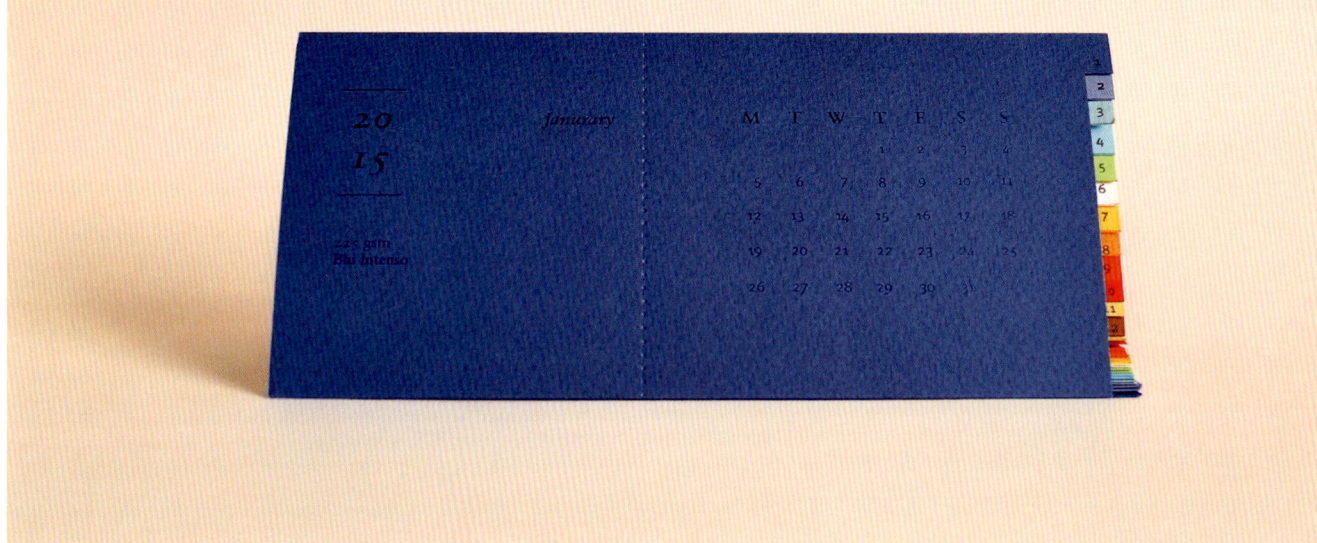

DESIGN
Danny Tsai

DESIGN AGENCY
Biaugust

Dragon Year Calendar

The idea for this design derived from dragon's scales. The outer form could be turned into a decorative frame around the card, and people could collect rubber bands and wrap them around the card. This made the calendar reusable even after the year had passed -- it could even be turned into a word game!

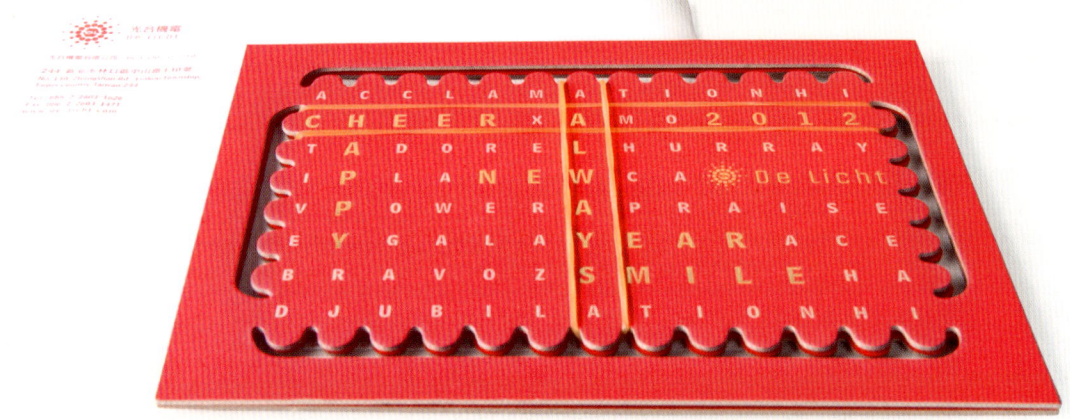

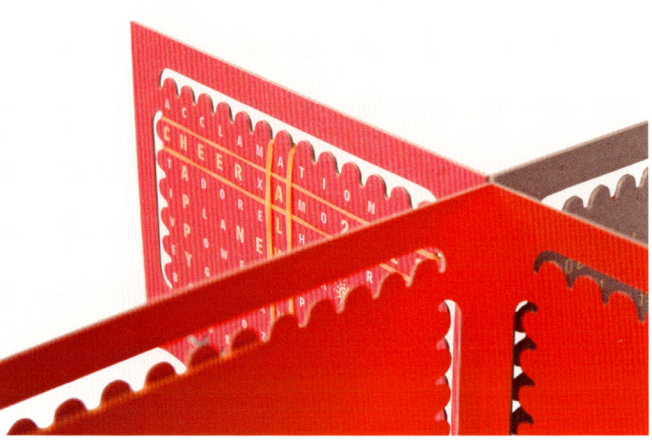

DESIGN AGENCY
Biaugust

Bird & Tree

The combination of tree and bird displayed the insistency of the wooden furniture brand on environment protection and reforestation. Besides than the emphasis on symbiosis in nature, the tree calendar had an inner magnet that could turn it into an organizational tool as well.

YCN Student Competition 2014 / Fedrigoni Calendar 2015 "LANDSCAPE"

This project was a flat desktop calendar created for the YCN Student Competition 2014. AngesMJ produced a clear, straight-forward calendar using the Sans Culottes typeface for the names of months and weekdays. The "LANDSCAPE" concept was based on the combination of rectangular shapes of the colorful pages that represented each month with their torn top edge, which created an abstract landscape when layered on each other. The composition of expressive shapes created a unique, natural character, which reflected the recycled and reused philosophy of the Woodstock range of the papers for Fedrigoni calendar 2015.

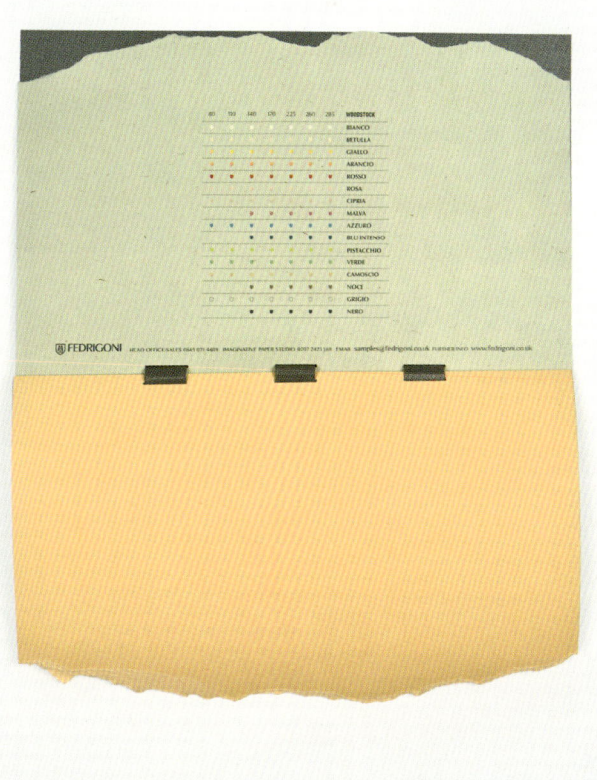

DESIGN AGENCY
Biaugust

Time is a Gift

This calendar was designed for leukemia patients. Biaugust applied the concept "time is a gift" to this work, rolling the 108 month (or 10 year) calendar inside a 10x10cm square box. The total length of the calendar was 12 meters. Each month was given a different visual design with the hope that it would make patients feel each day was distinguished from the other when they unraveled the roll.

DESIGN
Lili Thury

Planet Calendar / 2013

Designer Lili Thury made a planet calendar, wherein the planets were coupled with different months. Every planet was also associated with a metal. The designer's intention was to suggest the metallic character of the planets by using creative papers and yarn. Each month was placed separately in a bag which contained evocative elements, prints, and a foldout calendar, which could be used as a poster. The designer used yarn to link the dates, evoking a sense of the dates as constellation and enhancing the interstellar atmosphere of the calendar.

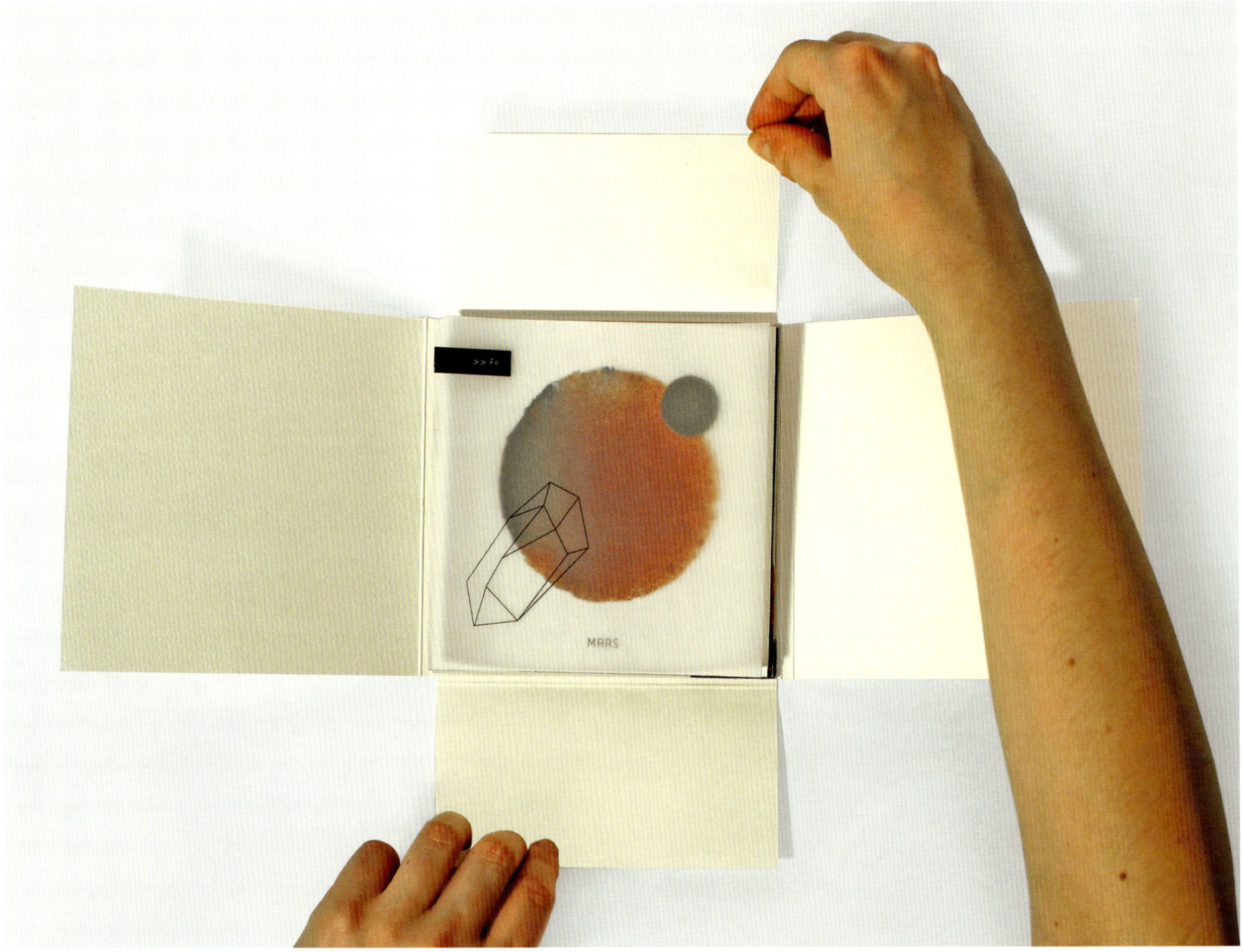

DESIGN AGENCY
Biaugust

Tea Life

Biaugust developed this calendar inspired by the concept of a "tea tree." The tea family's expressions and actions under the tree change as the monthly calendar progresses and the seasons change, as reflected by the tree. The whole work acted to depict a happy life with tea.

DESIGN
Takahiro Sugawara

ART DIRECTOR
Katsumi Tamura

COPYWRITER
Toshiyuki Nagamatsu

Botanical Life

Botanical life was a calendar that highlighted the beauty of plant life in a single sheet. The user could open the sheet and set it on the base to enjoy a variety of plant pop-ups. The high-quality design had the power to modify space and transform the minds of its users. Every aspect of the calendar, whether viewing it, holding it, or using it, offered comfort to the user. They were imbued with lightness and an element of surprise, and enriched whatever space they were placed in. These original products were designed with the concept of "Life with Design" in mind.

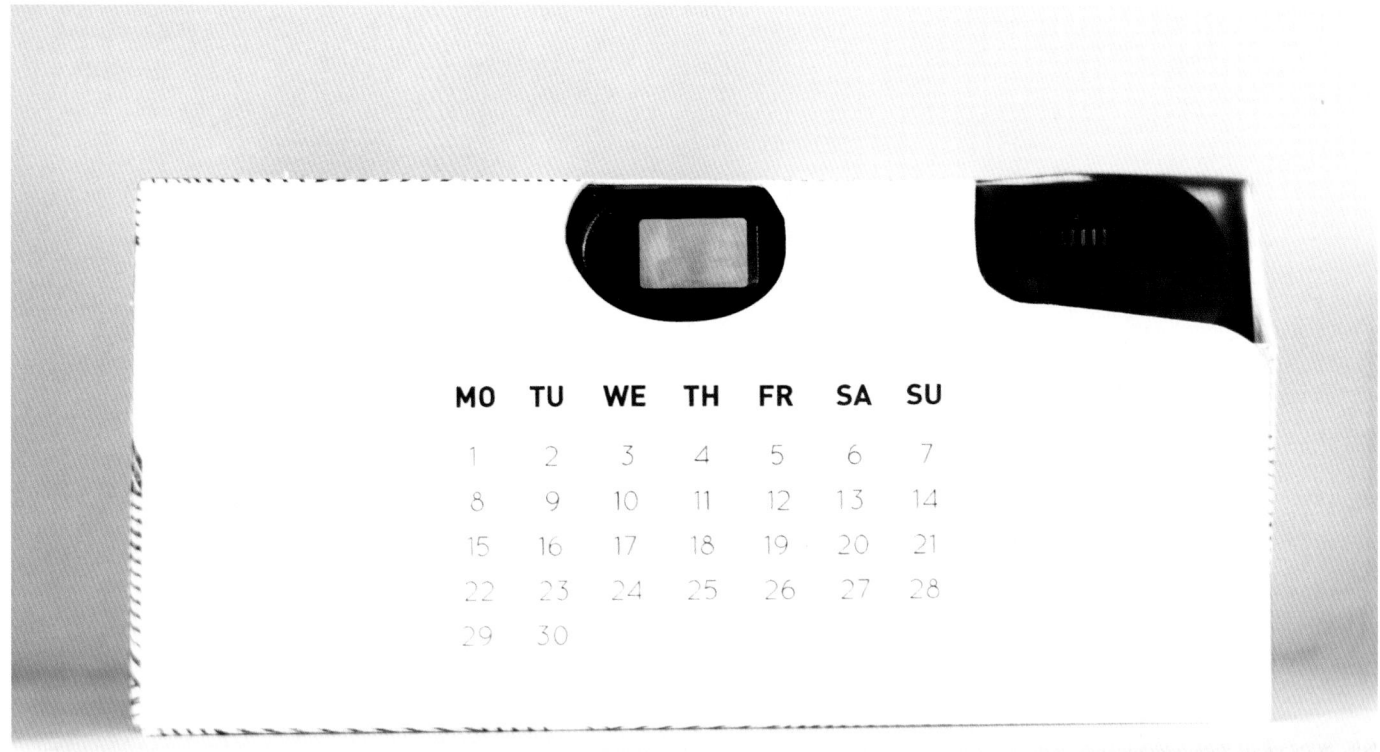

365 – Memory Calendar

This was a calendar based on the 365 days photo project: one photo for each day and 365 photos for the year. The user of this calendar would receive 12 cameras and 12 empty booklets, presented in a so-called "type case." There was one camera for every month plus a matching booklet. The user took a photo every day, which, after developing the film, could be pasted into the booklet that accompanied the month.

DESIGN AGENCY
Muschi & Licheni Design Network

Numerario (venti numeri 365 giorni)

The *Numerario* was a tool designed to order time in a temporary way. It was a table calendar excluding days, months, and years, and therefor was always on time. It was divided into ten units that people could combine with different numbers that had been designed specifically for the calendar. It was available in four languages: French, English, Italian, and German.

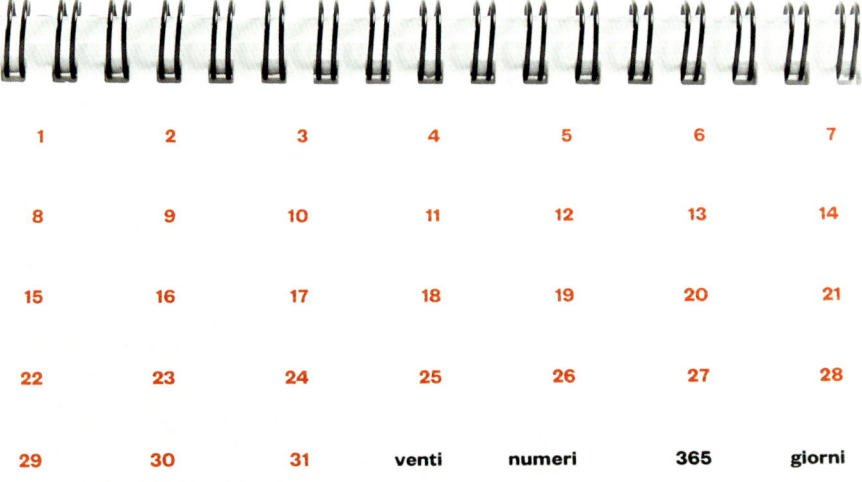

DESIGN
Kara Collins

TYPOGRAPHY
Kara Collins

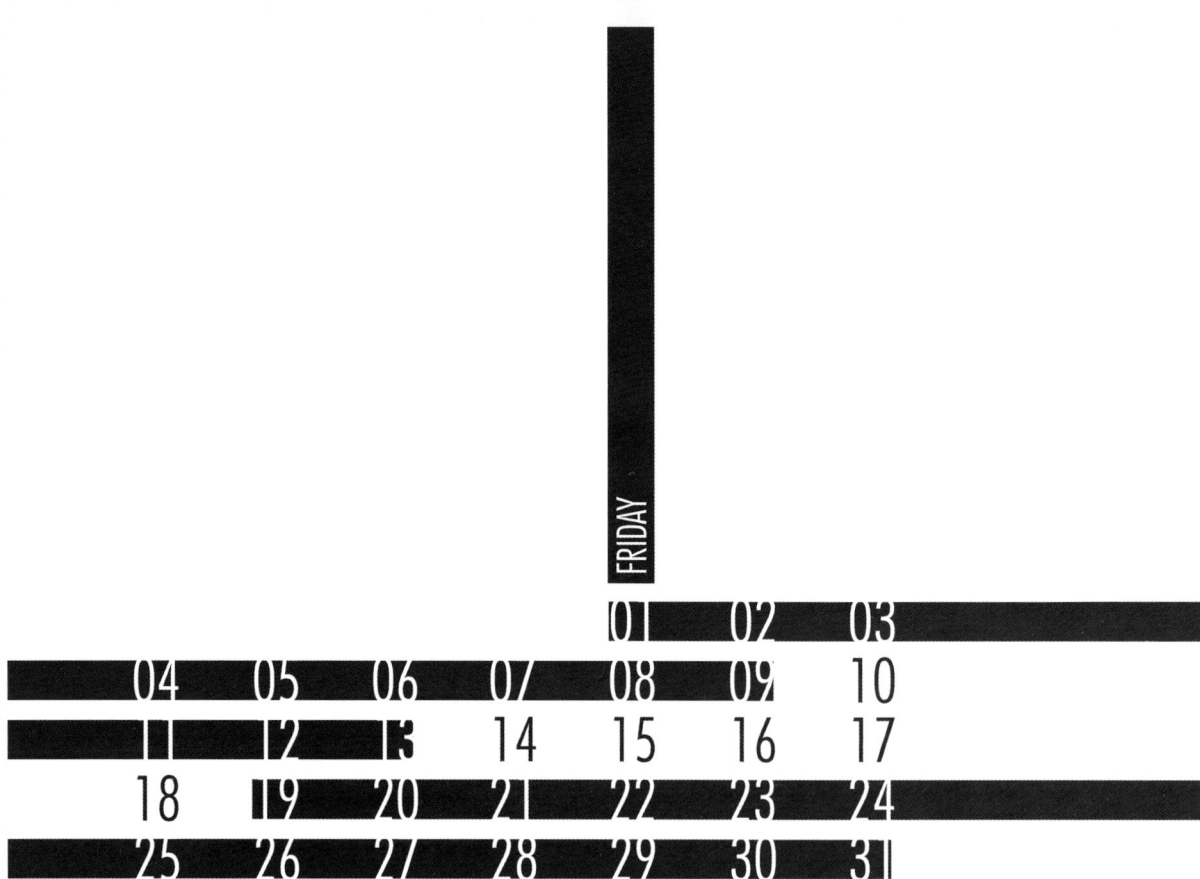

Calendar: Strictly Type

The object of this project was to design a twelve-month calendar using only type. A different type treatment, or a combination of type treatments, was used for each month: i.e. in January, the typeface varied in size, while in October it was cropped.

20**MAY**14

THURSDAY 01 02 03 07 08 09 10
04 06 15 17
11 13 22 24
18 05 20 14 29 16
25 27
12 21 23
19 28 30
26

20**JUNE**14

2 3 4 5 6
8 9 10 11 12
SUNDAY 1
13
14 15 16 17
19 20 21 22
18 23 24 25 26 27
28
29 30 31

SATURDAY 1
4 8
7 11 15
14 18 22
21 25 29
28 5 12 2
19 9
26 16
6 23
13 30
20 3
27 10
17
24

20**NOVEMBER**14

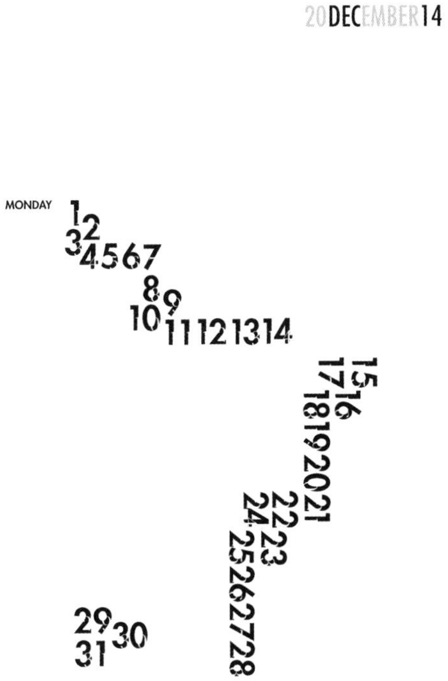

20**DECEMBER**14

MONDAY 1 2
3 4 5 6 7
8 9
10 11 12 13 14
15 16
17 18 19 20 21
22 23
24 25 26 27 28
29 30
31

DESIGN
Dimitris Anapliotis

DESIGN AGENCY
DESIGNCLUB Creative Art Works

2014 Calendar

The main focus of this calendar was to make it easy to use. Designer Dimitris Anapliotis worked with basic shapes in order to create the capital letters for each month and the number "2014". Moreover, he decided to "play" with black and grey in order to create a cooler design instead of the strict black and white contrast. For Sundays, Dimitris used magenta, which was the main color of DESIGNCLUB logo.

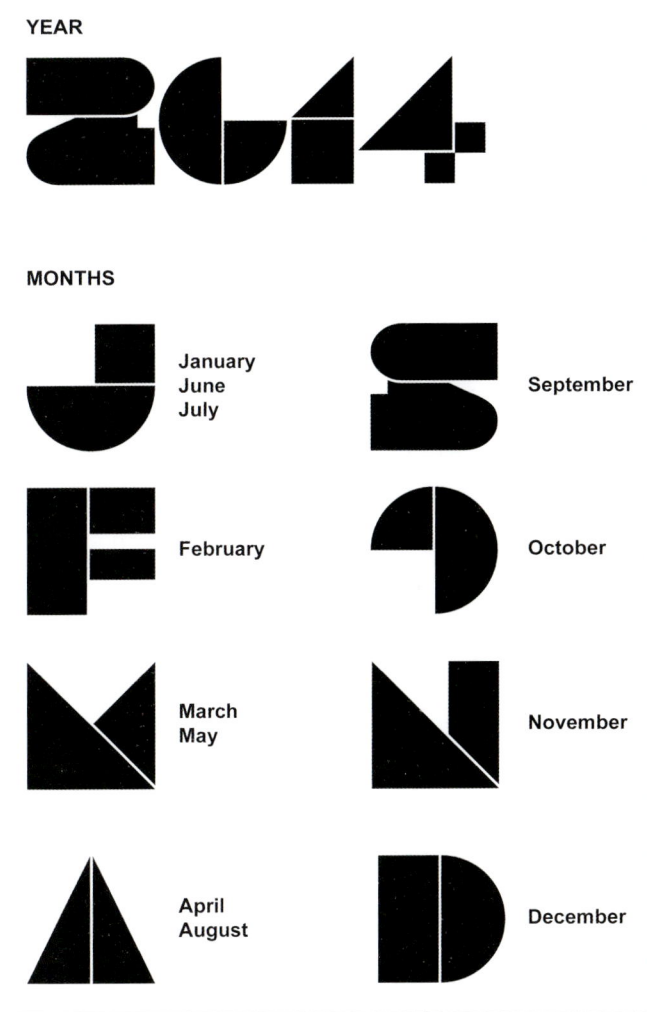

DESIGN
Justyna Koc

Calendar About the Sea

This project was a result of an exercise in Typography Studio of Grazyna Lange in Academy of Fine Arts in Warsaw. The task was to visually interpret the sea in a calendar. Using only a print, a bowl of water, and a camera, designer Justnya Koo created these interesting results.

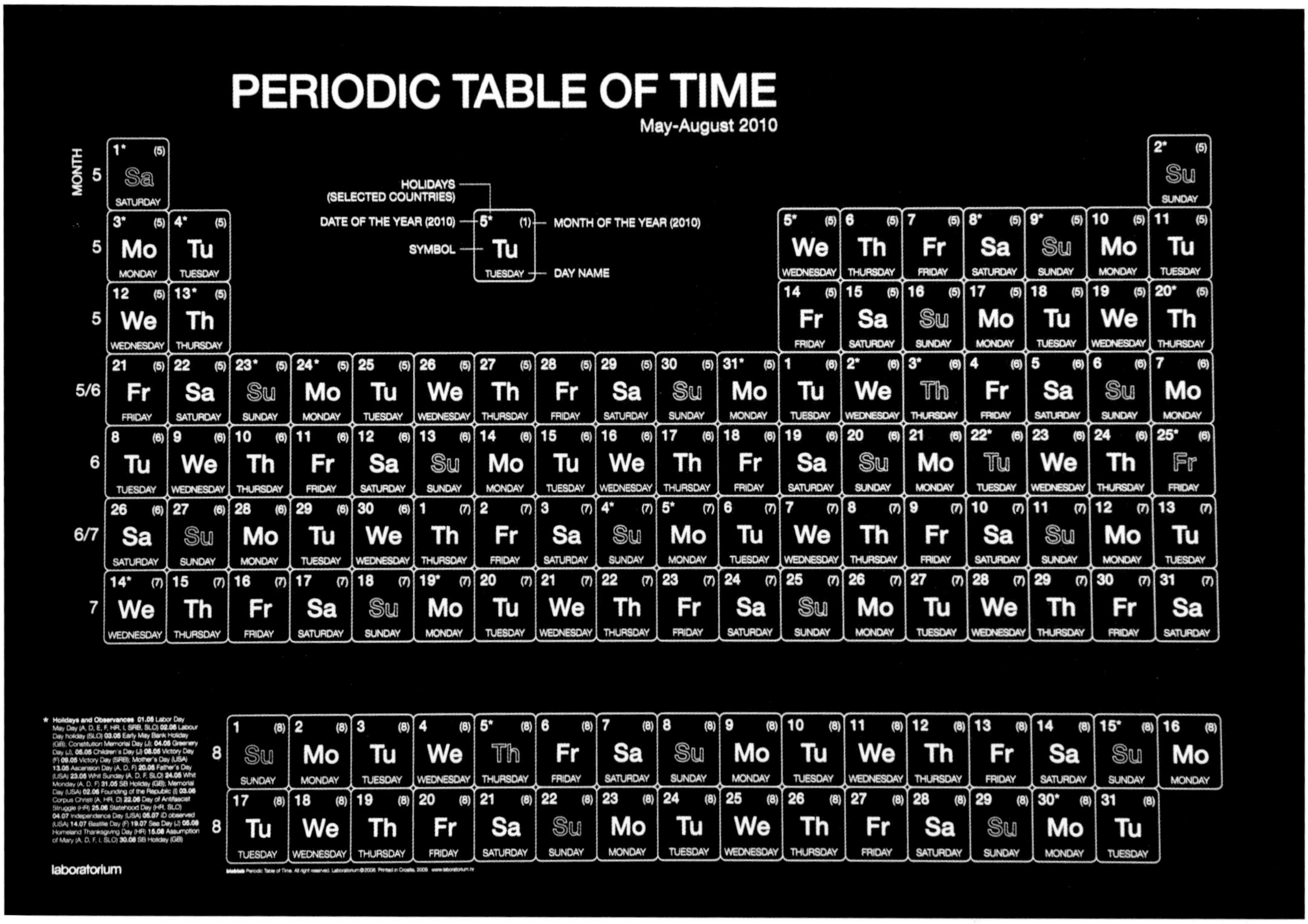

DESIGN
Ivana Vucic

DESIGN AGENCY
Hamper Studio / Laboratorium

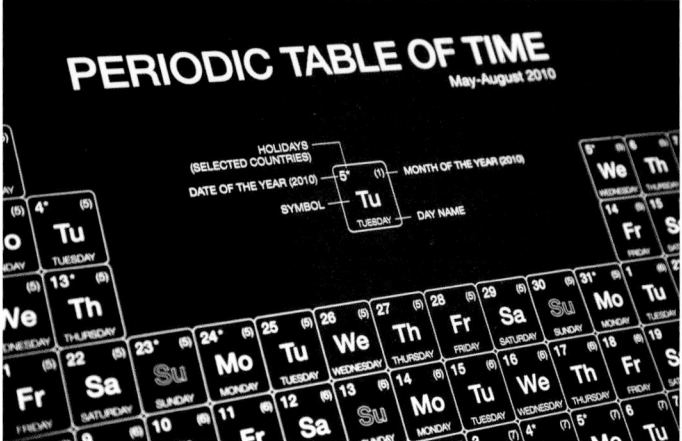

Periodic Table of Time

Periodic Table of Time (PTT) was a three-part calendar designed following Mendeleev's strict principle which helped people organize their daily life, as well as their future. It was an ideal planner for hard science lovers and world travellers. Originally PTT calendar was designed as a Christmas gift for Laboratorium studio clients and friends. The scientific "laboratory look" was used to emphasize experimental nature of studio Laboratorium.

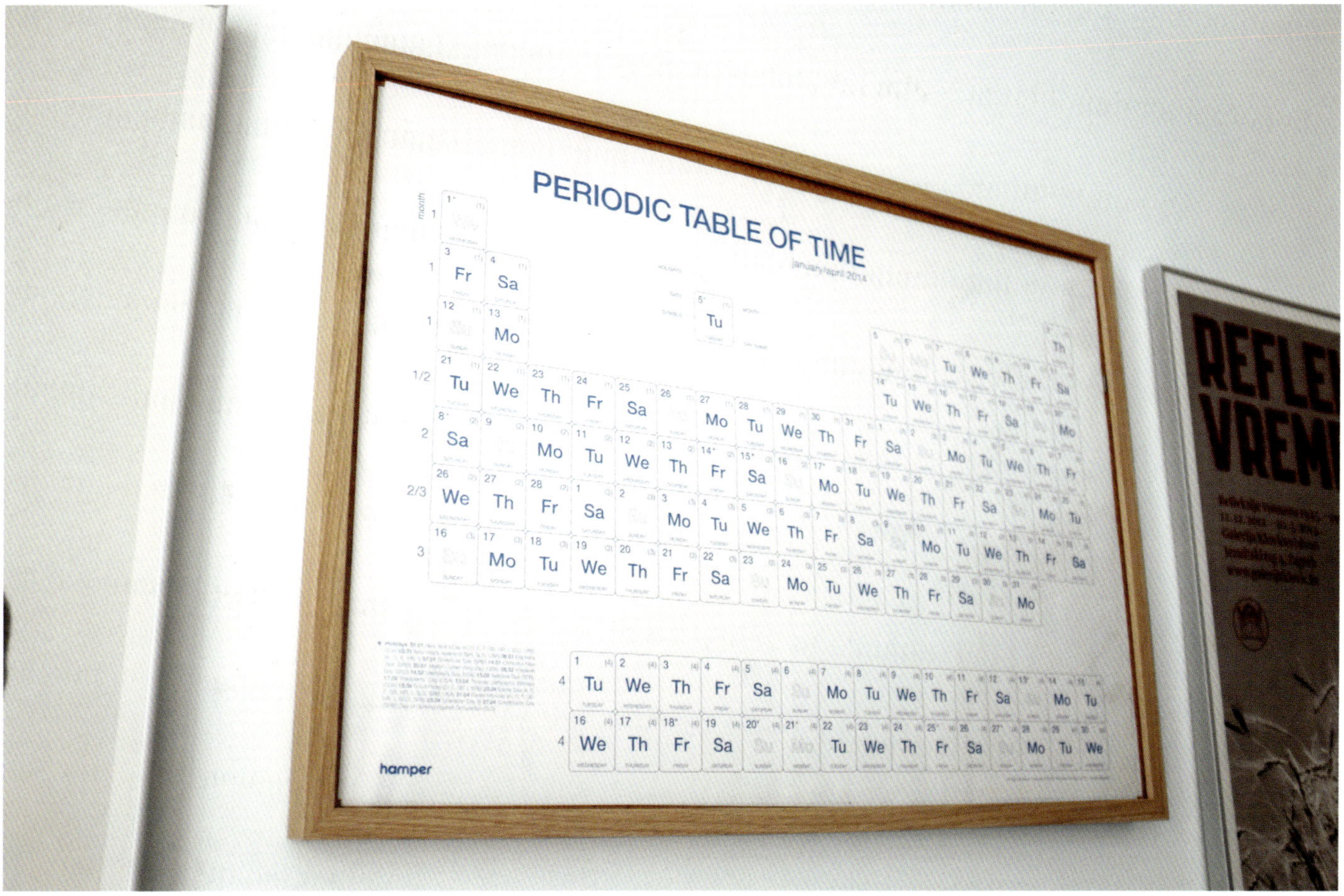

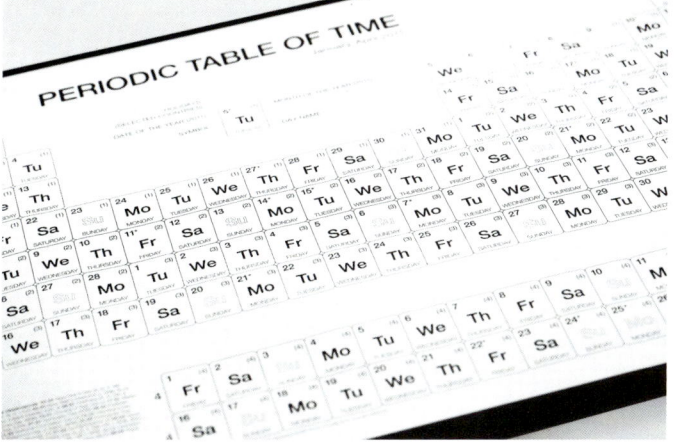

DESIGN GIMMICK
Jennita Shah Jennita Shah

"Pull Up Yourself to Face New Challenges" Calendar

This was an interactive calendar designed for the month of January. It displayed the resolutions for the New Year in the form of pull-in and pull-out tabs.

DESIGN	CONCEPT	HANDMADE SCREEN PRINTING
Cristina Bianchi	Cristina Bianchi	Cristina Bianchi and Emanuel Jesse

Two Thousand Ten

Two Thousand Ten was a limited edition handmade screen printed calendar designed as a Christmas present. Without buying anything new, designer Cristina Bianchi used some old forgotten curtains, several buttons, and a few wood clothes hangers to make this project.

DESIGN
Alesia Yurtsevich

NOVEMBER

1 2 3 4 5 6 7 8 9 10 11 12 13 14 15 16 17 18 19 20 21 22 23 24 25 26 27 28 29 30

Calendar "Graphic Design"

The theme of this calendar was graphic design. Designer Alesia Yurtsevich depicted her professional occupation as a designer on it, while making it as minimalist as possible. A black and white photo of the equipment that has helped her most in the design processes was centered on white sheets, with a single capital letter signifying the month imposed over it in a bright color. The shapes of the equipment also intentionally matched the contours of the letters.

AUGUST

1 2 3 4 5 6 7 8 9 10 11 12 13 14 15 16 17 18 19 20 21 22 23 24 25 26 27 28 29 30 31

MARCH

1 2 3 4 5 6 7 8 9 10 11 12 13 14 15 16 17 18 19 20 21 22 23 24 25 26 27 28 29 30 31

OCTOBER

1 2 3 4 5 6 7 8 9 10 11 12 13 14 15 16 17 18 19 20 21 22 23 24 25 26 27 28 29 30 31

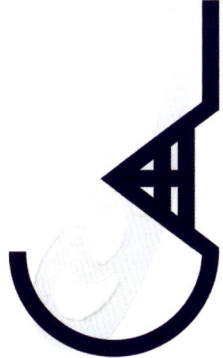

JANUARY

1 2 3 4 5 6 7 8 9 10 11 12 13 14 15 16 17 18 19 20 21 22 23 24 25 26 27 28 29 30 31

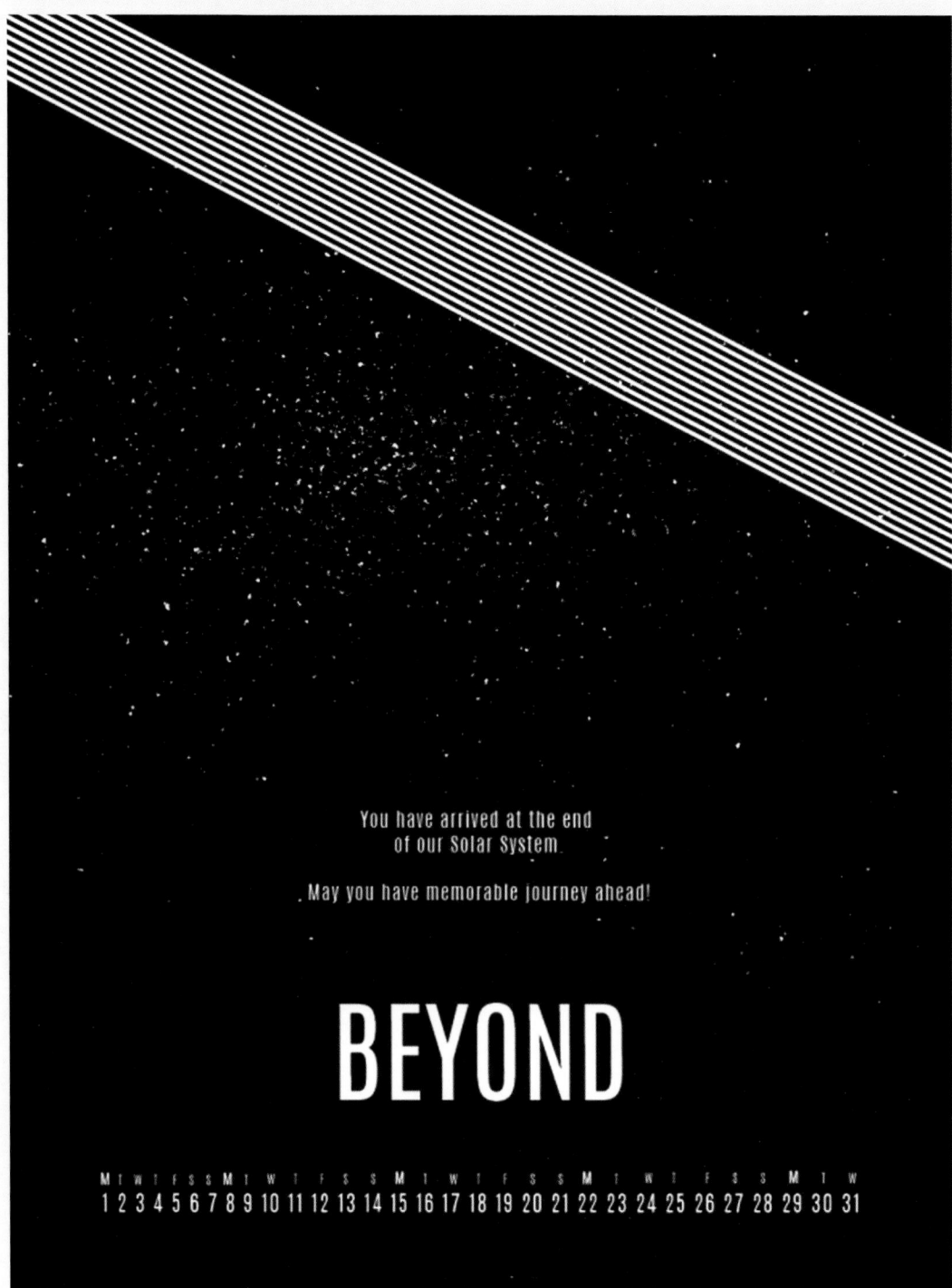

Planetary Calendar 2014

People are always intrigued and curious about the universe. Every human undertakes a journey, and a calendar is there to tell each and every one of us how long our journey has been. Everyone is on a journey through their own life, but the same goes for the planets, the solar system, and our entire universe. This calendar was based on our solar system and the 365 days in a year. Bianca Luyt designed the planets geometrically, according to what she imagined our planets might look like. She kept the natural color schemes of the planets, moon, and sun in order to keep them recognizable. At times it can be hard for humans to image something so incredibly big, so she added a few numerical facts under every planet. Bianca removed the traditional format of calendar months and arranged the dates in lines to keep the design's simplicity. She hoped to encourage the viewer to look ahead at the year to come rather than back behind them, and to see the coming days as an adventure leading to more to discover in both life and in our immense universe.

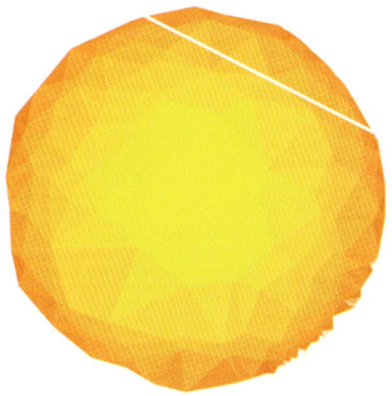

Distance from Earth: 149,597,900 km
Mean Radius: 695,508 km
Volume: 1,409,272,569,059,860,000 km³
Mass: 1,989,100,000,000,000,000,000,000,000 kg

SUN

M T F S S M T W T F S S M T W T F S S M T W T F S M T W T F
1 2 3 4 5 6 7 8 9 10 11 12 13 14 15 16 17 18 19 20 21 22 23 24 25 26 27 28 29 30 31

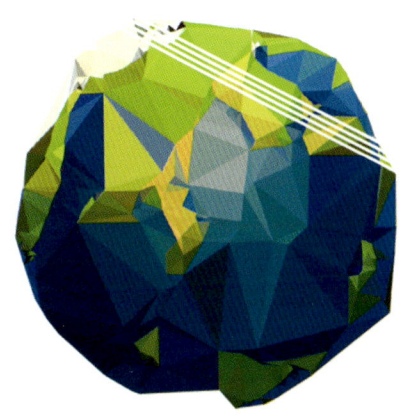

Orbit Size: 149,598,262 km
Mean Radius: 6371.00 km
Volume: 1,083,206,916,846 km³
Mass: 5,972,190,000,000,000,000,000,000 kg

EARTH

T F S S M T W T F S S M T W T F S S M T W T F S S M T W
1 2 3 4 5 6 7 8 9 10 11 12 13 14 15 16 17 18 19 20 21 22 23 24 25 26 27 28 29 30

Orbit Size: 108,209,475 km
Mean Radius: 6,051.8 km
Volume: 928,415,345,829 km³
Mass: 4,867,320,000,000,000,000,000,000 kg

VENUS

S S M T W T F S S M T W T F S S M T W T F S S M T W T F S S
1 2 3 4 5 6 7 8 9 10 11 12 13 14 15 16 17 18 19 20 21 22 23 24 25 26 27 28 29 30 31

Orbit Size: 57,909,227 km
Mean Radius: 2439.7 km
Volume: 60,827,208,724 km³
Mass: 330,104,000,000,000,000,000,000 kg

MERCURY

S S M T W T F S S M T W T F S S M T W T F S S M T W T F
1 2 3 4 5 6 7 8 9 10 11 12 13 14 15 16 17 18 19 20 21 22 23 24 25 26 27 28

DESIGN
Magdalena Strączyńska

Calendar Concordia Design

This was the first calendar project for Concordia Design. The original size of this calendar was 100x70cm, and it was printed on both transparent paper and lightly colored paper.

DESIGN
Julia Adelova

Multiply Calendar

More? Overlay? Multiplay? Bright? Disco? It was all done to make every month fun. This calendar was made for those people who regard weekend as the most important part of the week — it was easy to find (or lose) the thin type of the weekends, hidden and drowning in the "fat" work days.

DESIGN
Maria Musienko

ILLUSTRATION
Maria Musienko

Conceptual Series of Poster - Calendar "4392"

This series consisted of 12 calendars with pictures of the animals of the Chinese zodiac. Each calendar included 366 characters (symbols, personages), so the total number of characters in the entire series was 4392.

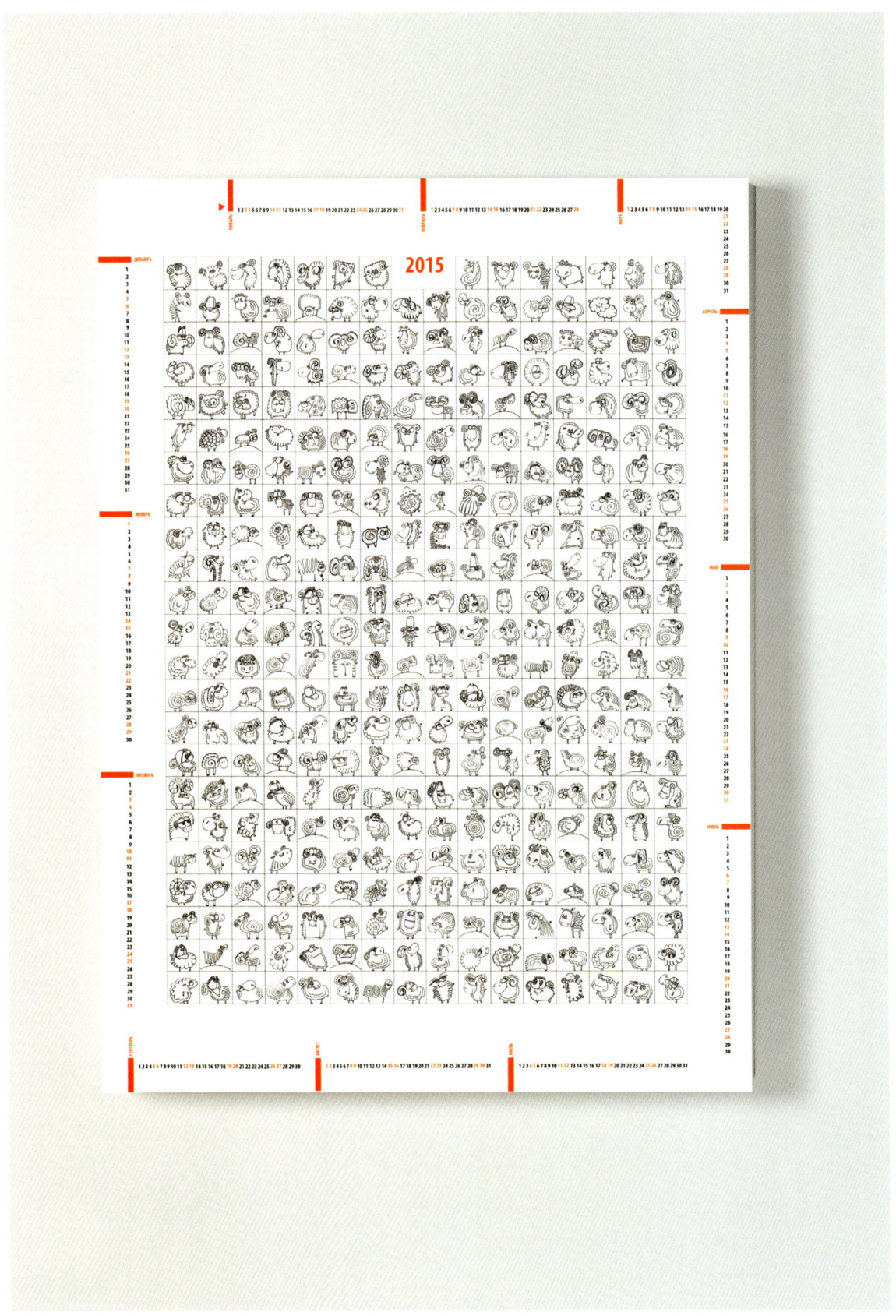

DESIGN AGENCY
Studio Lin

Studio Lin x Linco 2014 Calendar

The third calendar in a series of collaborations between Linco Printing (a NYC printer) and Studio Lin. The designer punched out weekends and holidays from one side of a French-folded folded sheet to reveal the interior printing.

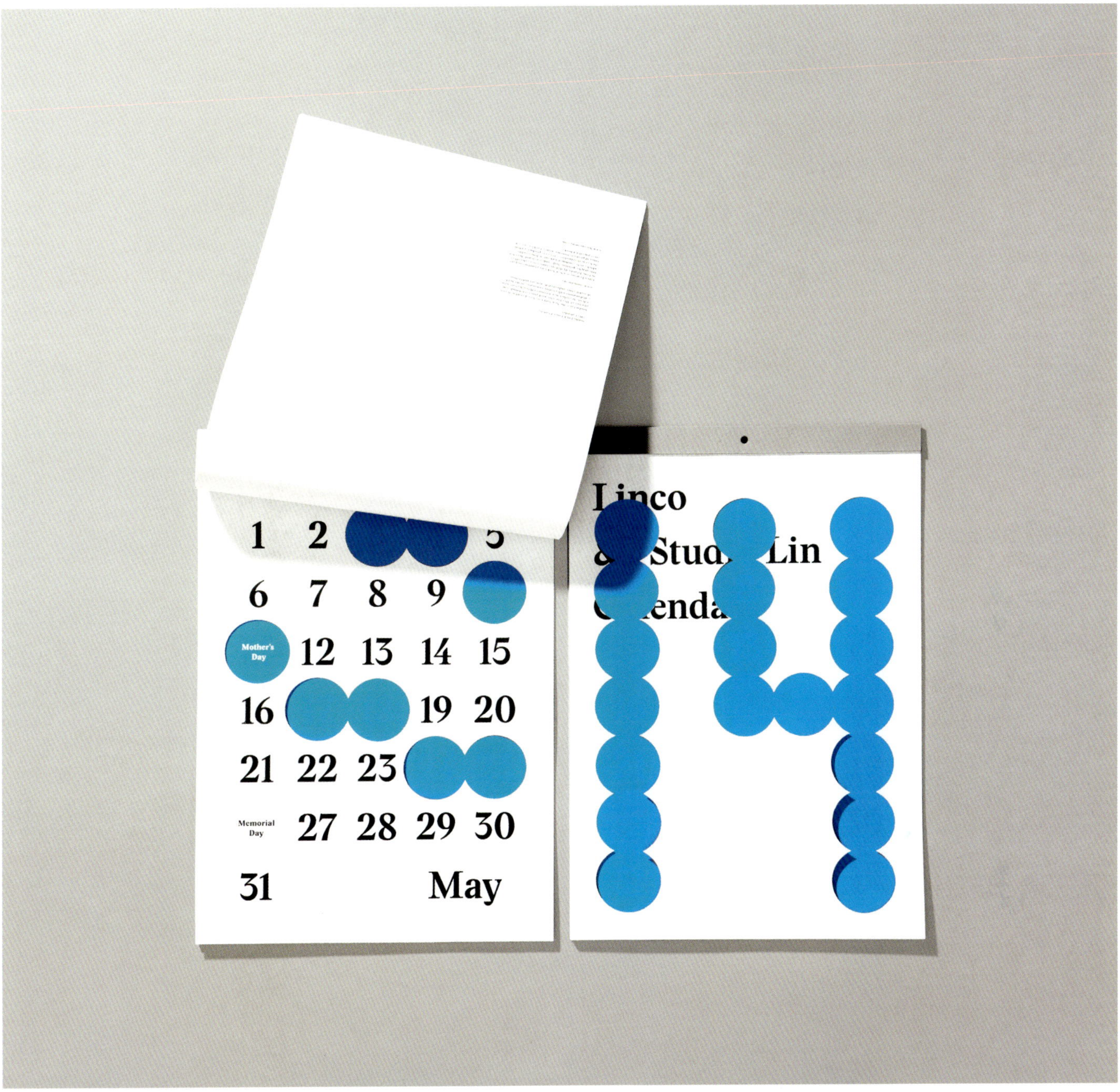

DESIGN
Iwona Przybyla

Embroidery Calendar

This work was a different approach to the idea of a calendar. It was aimed at people looking for new forms and solutions in their daily lives, and its goal was to be a design that would find a place both at home and work. The project featured the name of each month embroidered on paper and an unorthodox arrangement of the days of the week.

DESIGN
Gonçalo Campos

Dia Calendar

A calendar that allowed people to see the year pass more naturally, and let them interpret the passage of time in an intuitive way by adding one piece of the puzzle per day. The universal puzzle pieces allow for numerous expressions of how people see the year, how they personally relate to it, or how they wish it would be, by arranging and drawing with them any way they like.

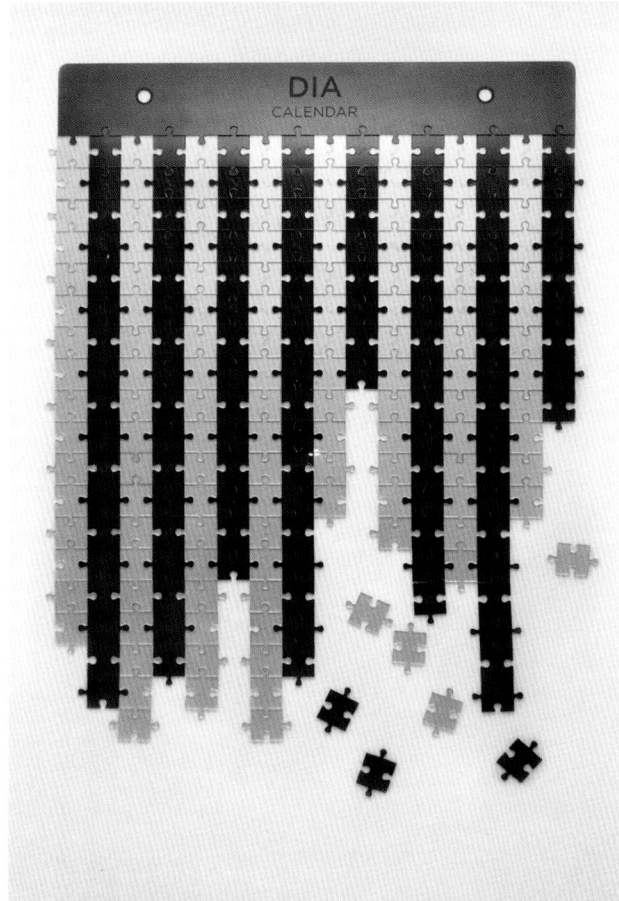

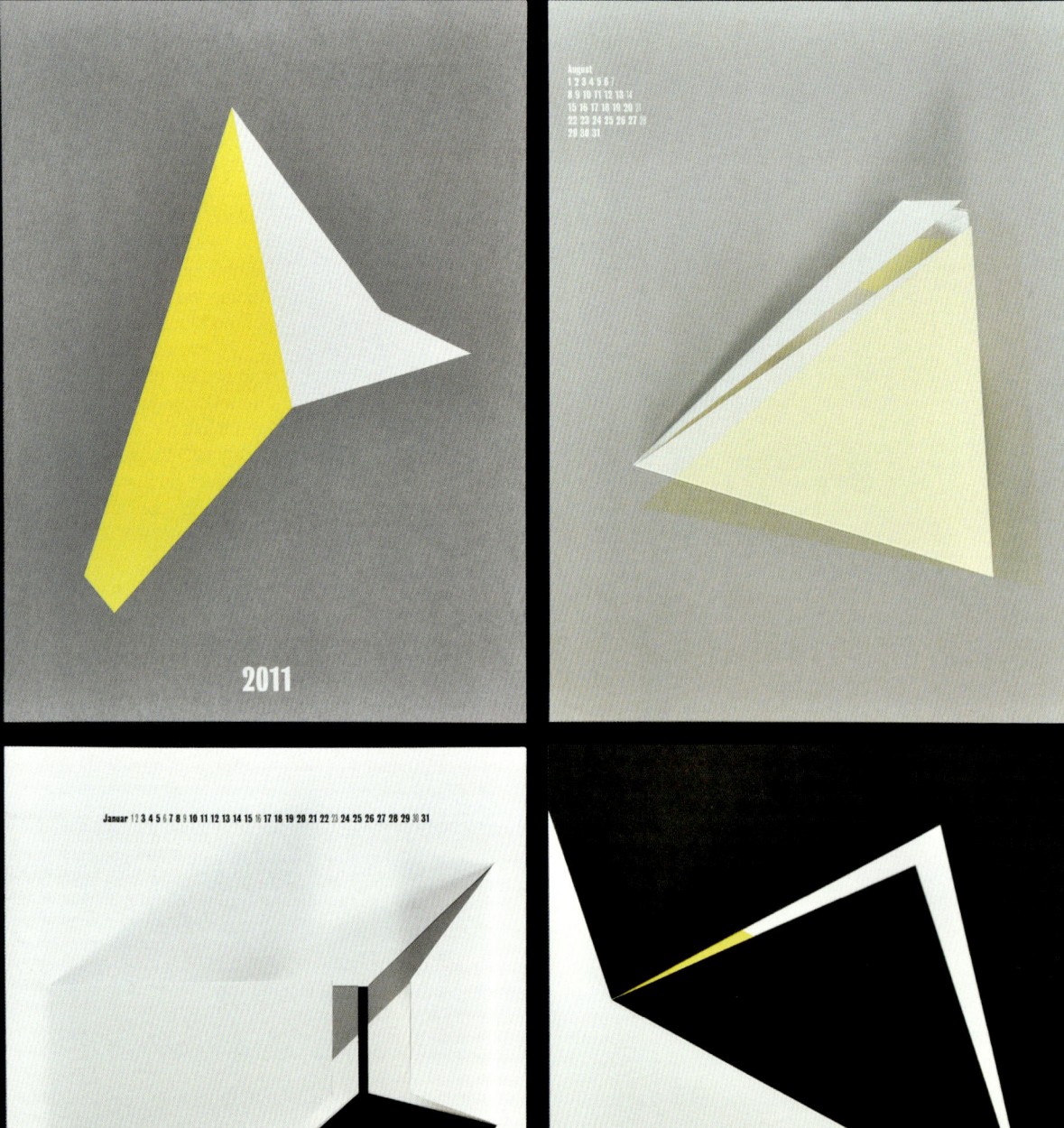

Mühleisen and Partner Calendar

Calendar design for the architecture firm Mühleisen & Partner. Each month of the year was a sheet of paper that was cut and scored, which could then be folded to create 3D shapes, revealing a preview of the forthcoming month that lies behind. This project was made in collaboration with artist Lisa Mühleisen.

September
1 2 3 4
5 6 7 8 9 10 11
12 13 14 15 16 17 18
19 20 21 22 23 24 25
26 27 28 29 30

Juli 1 2 3 4 5 6 7 8 9 10 11 12 13 14 15 16 17 18 19 20 21 22 23 24 25 26 27 28 29 30 31

April
1 2 3
4 5 6 7 8 9 10
11 12 13 14 15 16 17
18 19 20 21 22 23 24
25 26 27 28 29 30

Februar 1 2 3 4 5 6 7 8 9 10 11 12 13 14 15 16 17 18 19 20 21 22 23 24 25 26 27 28

DESIGN
Ermolaev Bureau

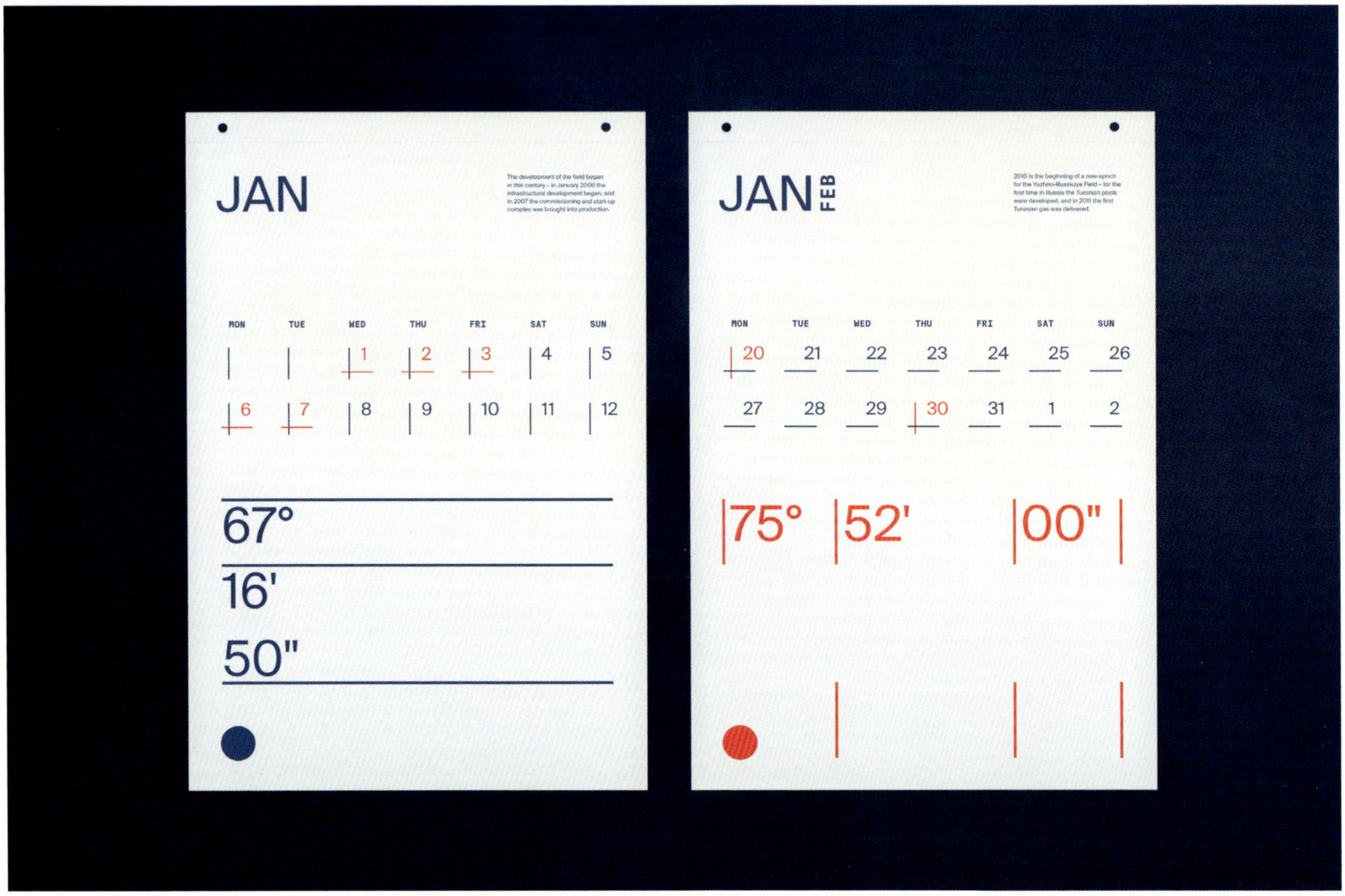

SNGP CALENDAR

This calendar was a part of a larger project to create a new visual identity for the Severneftegazprom company's souvenir products, as these products were the main means of the company's communication with partners and colleagues. This wall calendar was one of the first pieces created, and represented the new visual style to partners and employees of the company. One of the main points of the creative brief was to keep the initial shape of the logotype and company's colors, which was the reason why designer kept the colors (navy blue, blue and red), but selected new shades and adjusted the proportions of the logotype.

Saisonkalender 2014 für Obst & Gemüse

In September 2014, designer Cristina Bianchi moved from Italy to Austria. Once she crossed the Alps she realized how much the food and weather had changed, and decided to try to only eat locally and seasonally. She designed this poster calendar to display which fruits and vegetables were available in Austria at different times of the year. The calendar was a self-initiated project, and consisted of two layers of handmade screen printing on 290g orange paper.

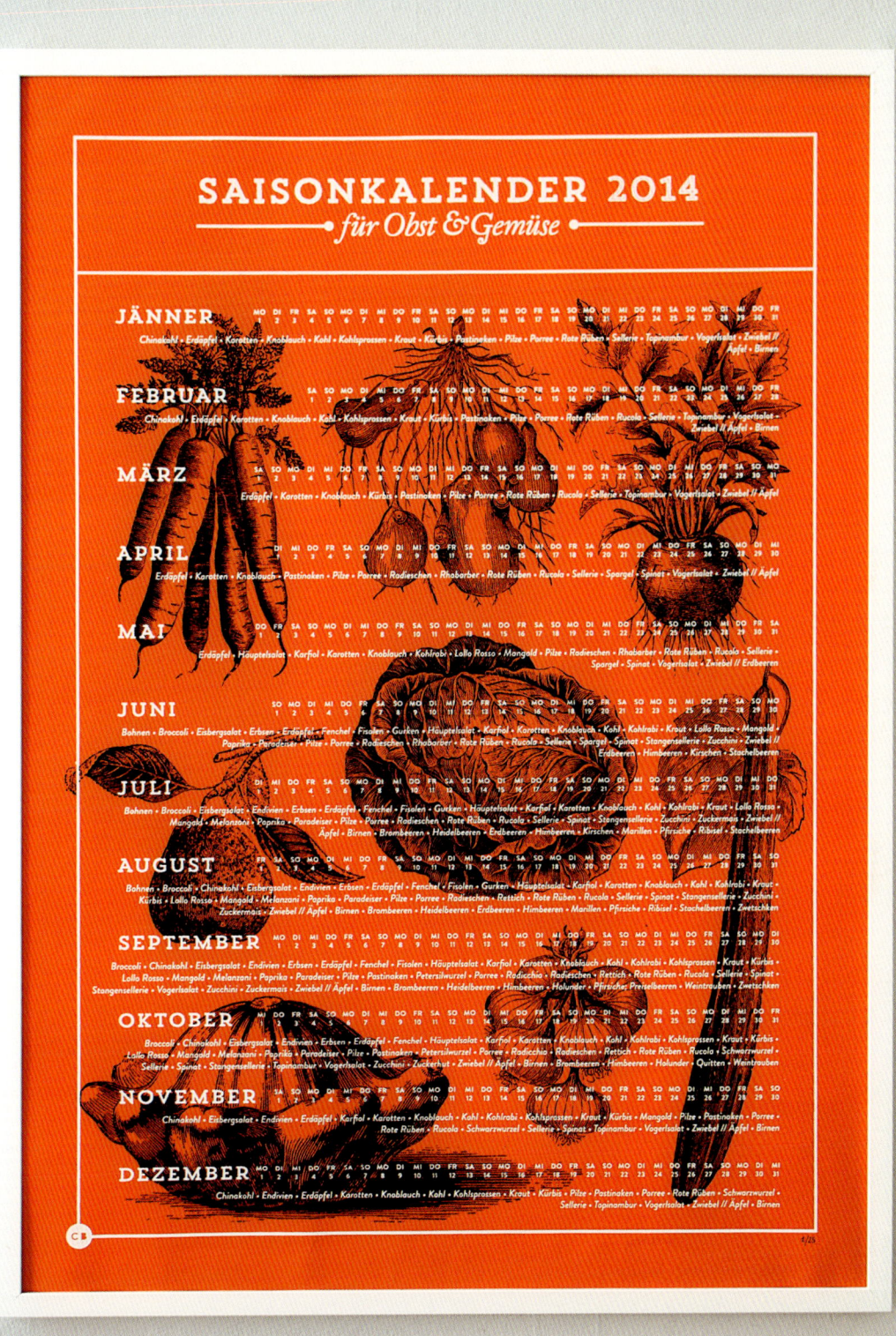

Calendar for the Firefighters

This project was Agata Bujko's school project for her first year of undergraduate studies in lettering typography at the Academy of Fine Arts in Gdansk, Poland. Bujko focused on the image of fire, and tried to present how it worked, changed, and what it left behind. She also attempted to show the depth and potential in its ignition. This calendar is unlike the majority of calendars, in which days of the month are static and days of the week are presented in various places. Rather, this calendar begins the days of the month from the same location.

DESIGN
Jessie Ning

Life is a Presto Music Note Calendar

Time flies, and life moves at a *presto* tempo. The idea of life matching music notes inspired the design of this calendar. Each note represented a month; the number of days within a month defined the duration of the note. From music theory, a crossing stroke made an eighth note, and two strokes made a sixteenth note. By analogy, January, for instance, had 31 days (strokes) that made it an 8589934592th (2^{31+2}) note. The extremely short notes symbolized the fleeting nature of days and highlighted the metaphor: life is a *presto*.

DESIGN
Lihi Bar-Or

TYPOGRAPHIC לוח שנה
CALENDAR טיפוגרפי

Typographic Calendar

Calendar design composed of typographic and graphic elements. The idea was to show the flow of time. Each line eventually connected to the dates and days of the week that matched it. The overall result was one organic movement that wove the days together, rather than the traditional calendar that isolated one day from the next.

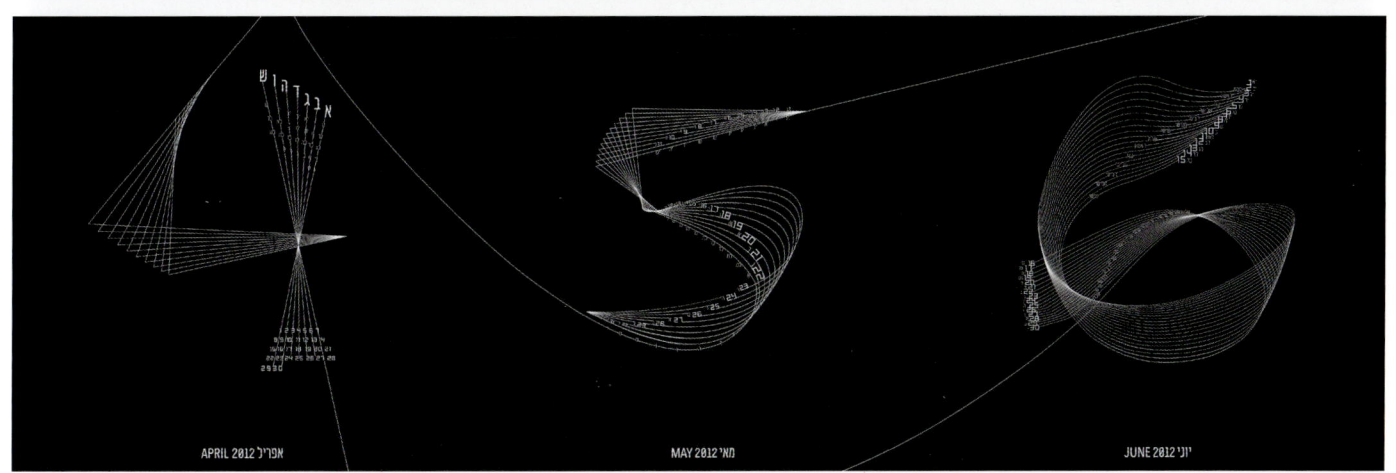

APRIL 2012 אפריל | MAY 2012 מאי | JUNE 2012 יוני

DESIGN
Vladimir Repin

Calendar<Motion>

The name of the calendar was inspired by the visual effect of movement that was caused by the use of different sized digits from small to large across the poster. They were placed in a special order to form the image of a moving arrow that went from the center of the poster to the edges. Designer Vladimir Repin used bright colors on a black background to cause a sparkling effect. The designer's goal with this project was to show the capabilities of time: it can seem to pulse or flow steadily, be smooth or stream past, but it is always inevitable.

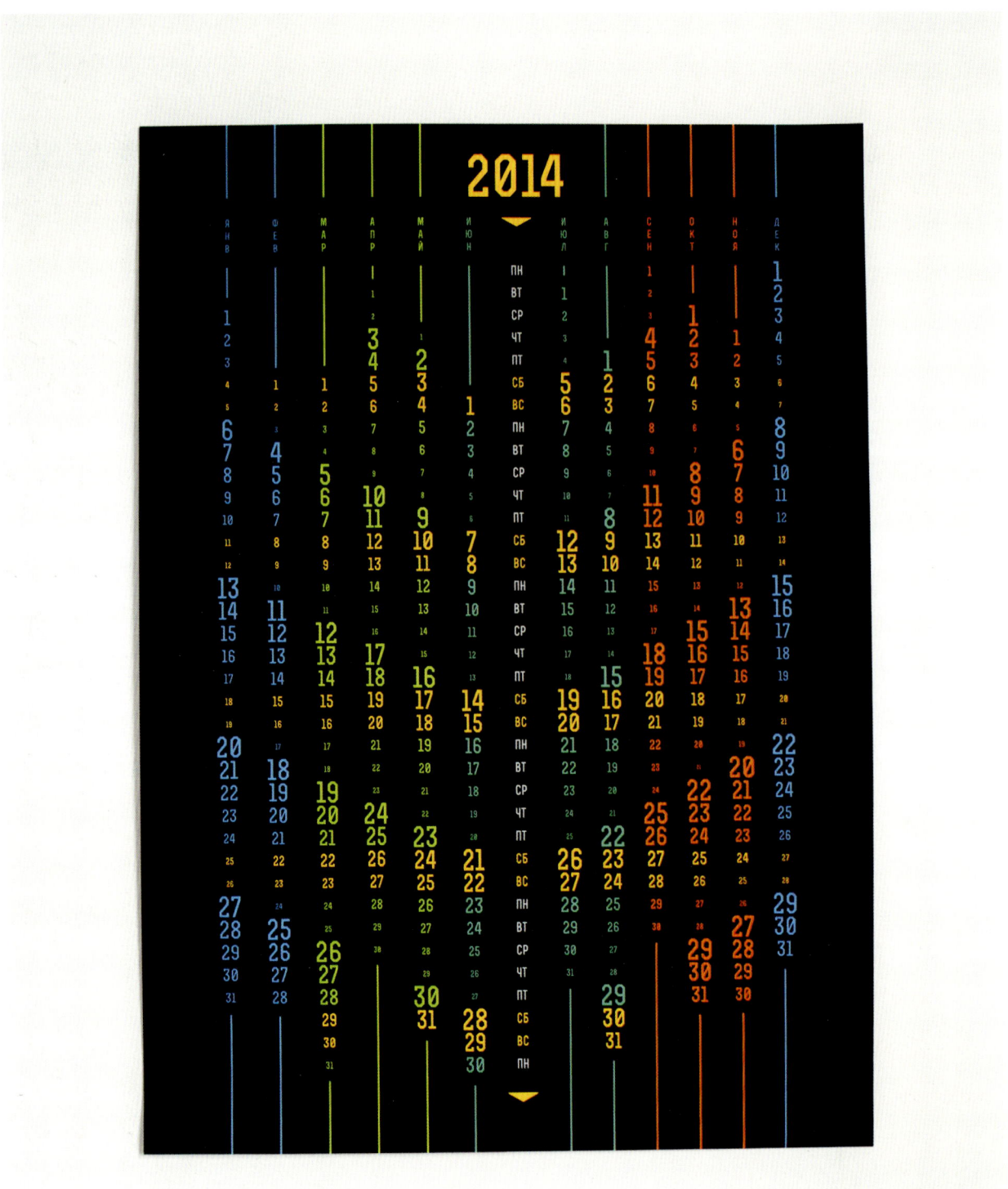

DESIGN
Maria Deligiorgi

PRINTING
Tind

PHOTOGRAPHY
Marilia Fotopoulou & Maria Deligiorgii

Night Calendar

This was a wall poster calendar that helped people count the nights of the year by being a poster during the day and only displaying the dates by night. The calendar absorbed light during the day and glowed in the dark, and worked under black light as well. It was silk screened with custom-made sparkling black or metallic purple ink; both versions were also printed with phosphorescent ink. The printing surfaces used were: Munken Polar 240 gr., recycled paper 240 gr., transparent or white sticker, transparent or White PVC, 0.3mm.

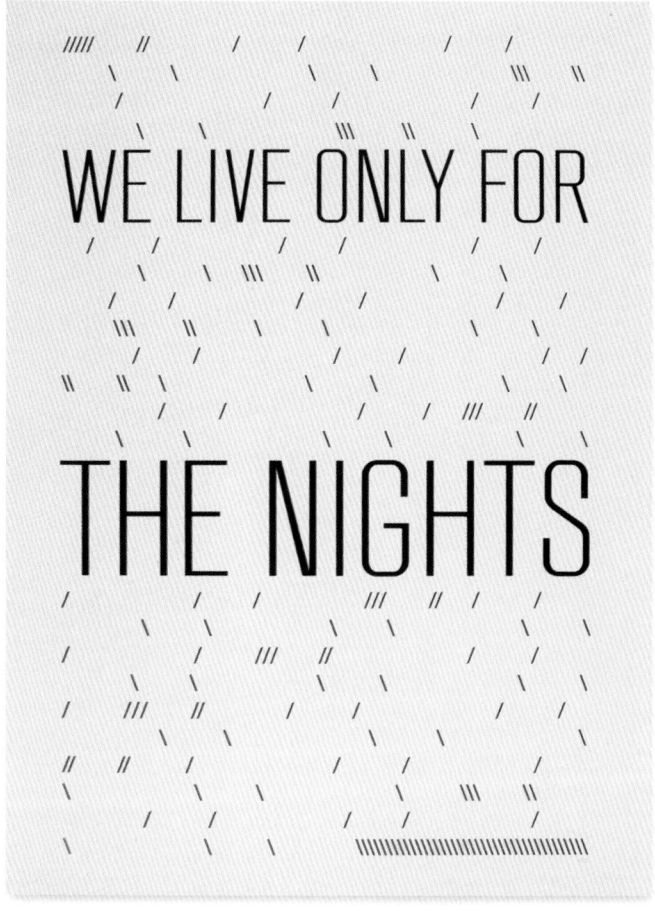

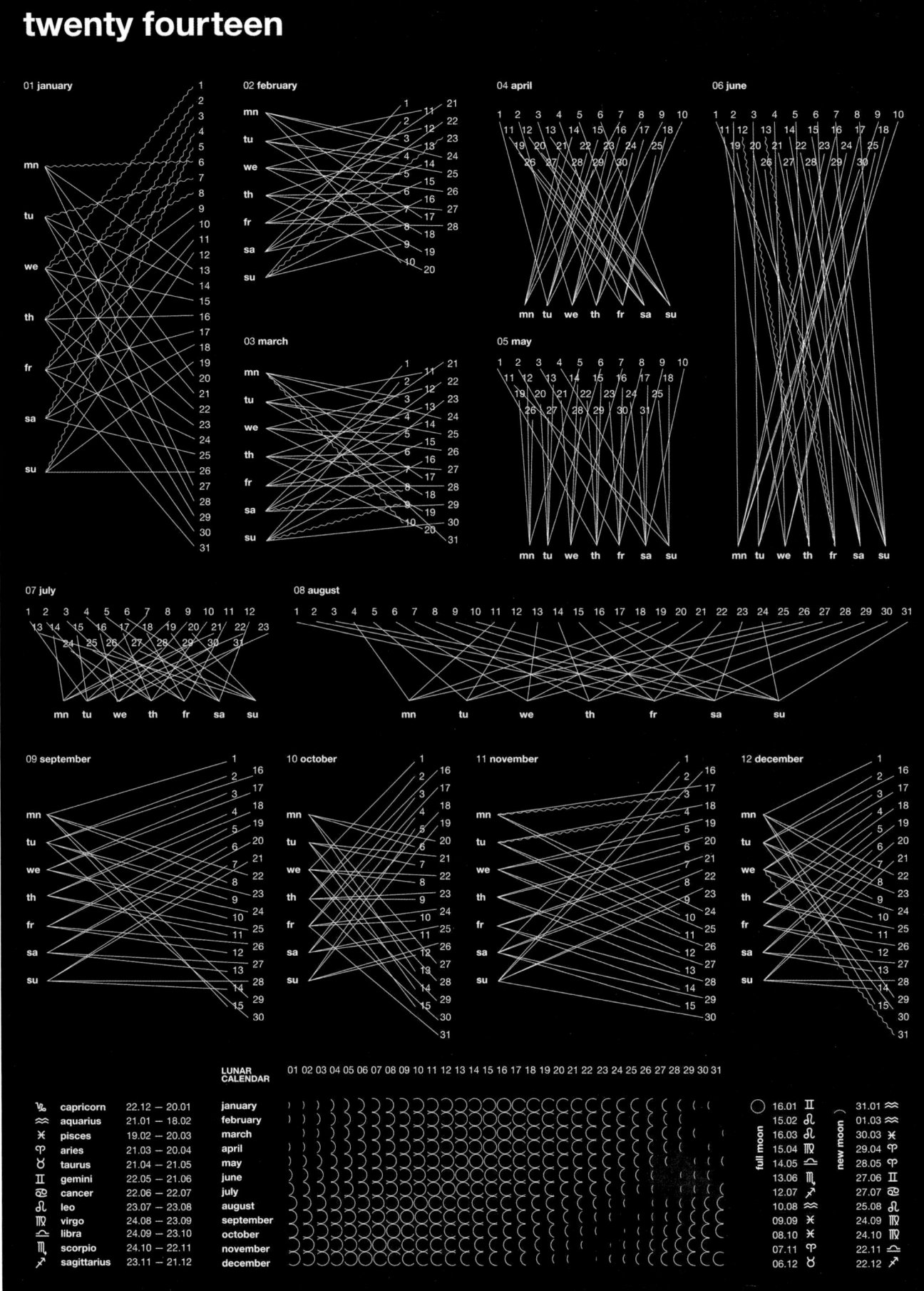

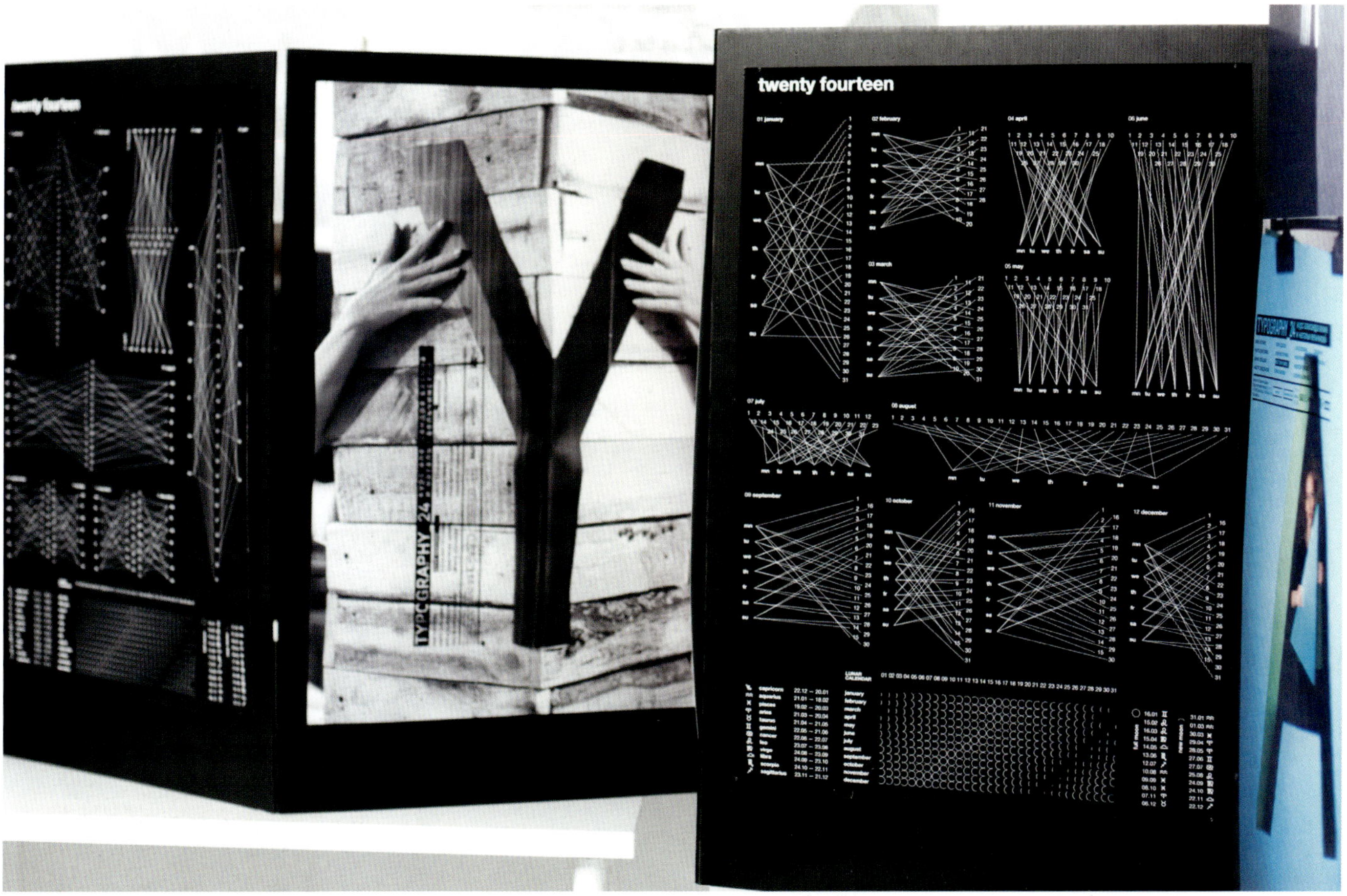

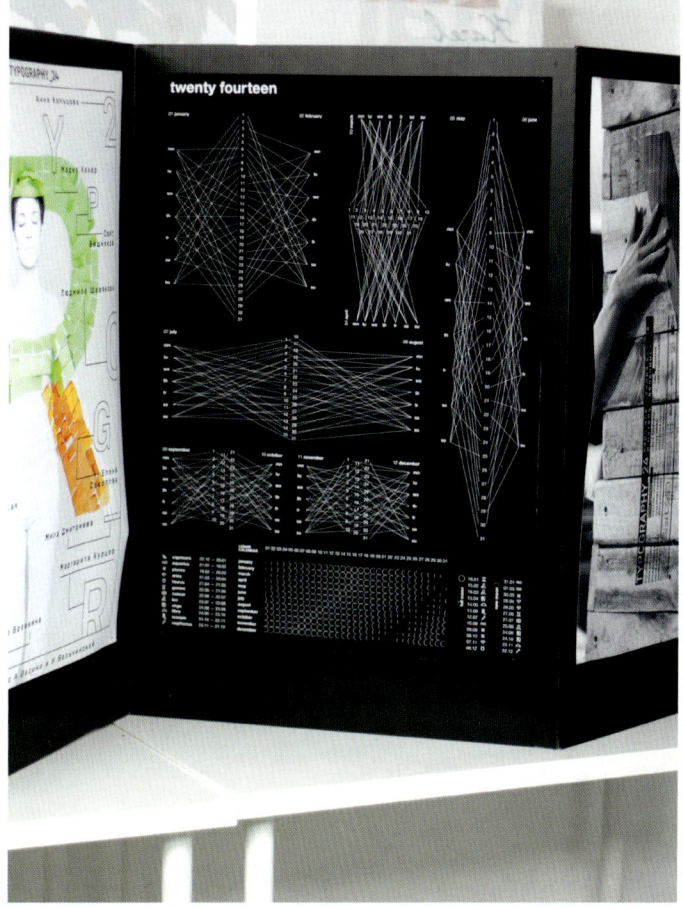

Black Calendar

What made this calendar different from other usual calendars was that its beauty caught attention from a distance, then inspired people to look closely to see all the details. The design made every month look like some kind of strange and unusual animal, and by the end of the last month of the year, the complex patterns of lines became visually dazzling.

DESIGN
Winnie Tan

TYPEFACE
Winnie Tan

The Simple Calendar

The Simple Calendar was conceived as a platform to showcase The Simple Typeface as a game of successful replicators that propagated itself into various forms of Latin alphabets, Chinese characters, and thematic icons. A single-weight, minimal, grid-based San-serif display, the Simple typeface was prudent with details, sturdy in form and geometrically-driven in design with an assortment of bilingual glyphs. In retrospect, The Simple Font was also realized to be well-catered for use in graphical information design in games and tournaments, logotypes, advertisements, and headlines.

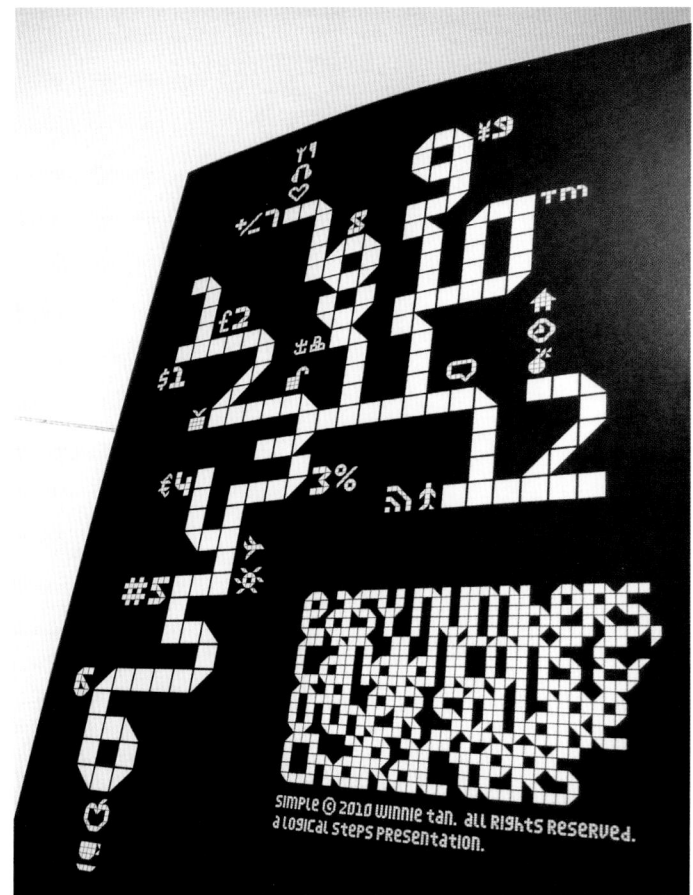

DESIGN
Chris Page

Die-cut Wall Calendar

This calendar consisted of thirteen loose sheets, one die-cut date sheet, and twelve colored month sheets. Each month sheet displayed dates of interest and the numbers 0, 4, 6, 8 and 9. It gave each sheet its own visual interest when viewed separately. When both the date and month sheets were placed together the date numbers were formed. Two bulldog clips held all sheets together.

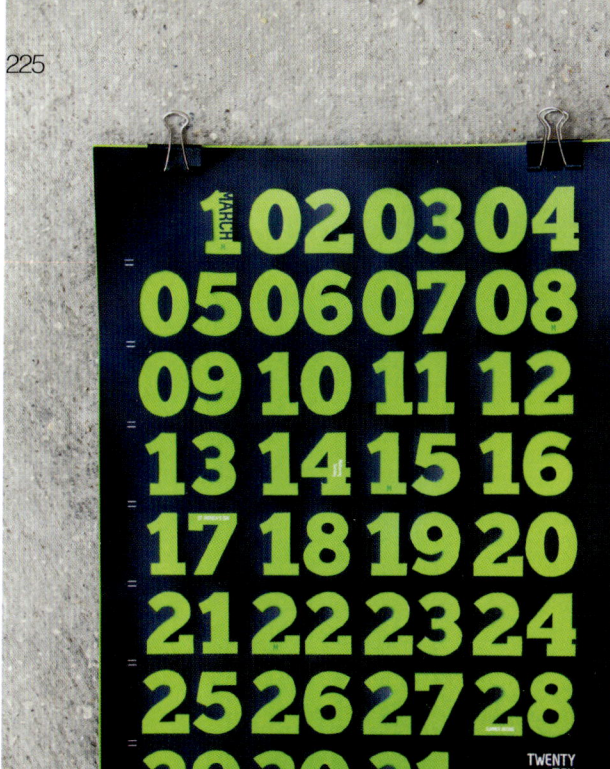

DESIGN
Sara Vrbinc

Calendar 2014

Designer Sara Vrbino created this project with the Henry David Thoreau quote "As if you could kill time without injuring eternity" as a conceptual starting point. She stretched every letter of the alphabet across six pages on grid of equivalent triangles. The user's task was to flick out each day's triangle as the day passed. As each month ran out, the user would see new letters in a variety of color combinations.

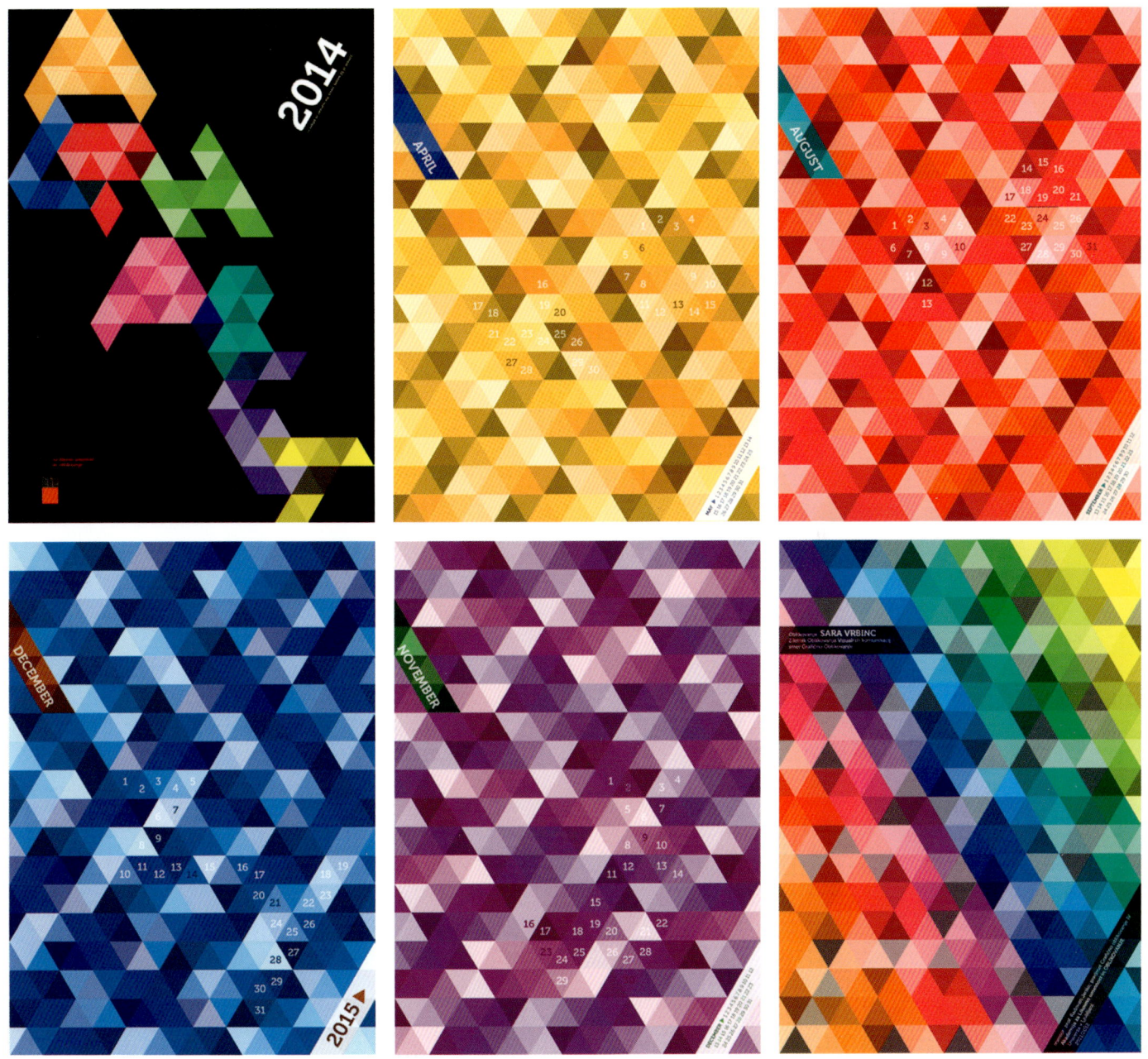

DESIGN AGENCY
Studio Lin

FAB 365 Calendar

Fab wanted to design a calendar and packaging to be given to their more than 4,000 vendors. Studio Lin's solution was an ultra colorful take on the Massimo Vignelli Max 365 calendar. The day could always be displayed no matter the year, giving this calendar long-lasting value. On the back of each page was an iconic product from each of Fab's many product categories. Studio Lin finished it off with custom printed reinforced tape to seal each of the boxes.

DESIGN AGENCY
Studio Lin

United Bamboo
2011 Cat Calendar

This 2011 calendar featured cats in miniature United Bamboo ready-to-wear collection. The calendar was a special luxury piece that showed United Bamboo as a funny and innovative fashion company.

3

1 / 2 / 3 / 4 / 5
6 / 7 / 8 / 9 / 10 / 11 / 12
13 / 14 / 15 / 16 / 17 / 18 / 19
20 / 21 / 22 / 23 / 24 / 25 / 26
27 / 28 / 29 / 30 / 31

6

1 / 2 / 3 / 4
5 / 6 / 7 / 8 / 9 / 10 / 11
12 / 13 / 14 / 15 / 16 / 17 / 18
19 / 20 / 21 / 22 / 23 / 24 / 25
26 / 27 / 28 / 29 / 30

4

APRIL
Name: Ziggy
Age: 1 ½ years old
Tail Measurement: 10"
Eye Color: Blue
Pet Peeve: Other animals, he thinks he's human.

Ziggy loves toys! He was returned to the pet store and I got him by fate.

Floral Print Mini Dress with Sarong Sleeve Detail (UMI1100)

2

FEBRUARY
Name: Oscar
Age: 6–8 years old
Tail Measurement: 12"
Eye Color: Green
Pet Peeve: Oscar does not like it when people blow air in his face, it messes up his pretty whiskers!

I didn't know he was blind until after I adopted him! He has cheated death twice! OMG!

Regatta Blazer with Striped Trim (UMV1100)
White Shirt Dress

Haircuts Calendar

This calendar had an interesting history. Once designer Julia Adelova was unhappy with her haircut. She knew about haircut calendars, and created this project to show the good and bad days for haircuts and other jobs involving hair. The red crosses on the calendar mark days that she didn't have any jobs with hair.

INDEX

A

Adrian Meseck
www.behance.net/adrian-meseck

Adrian F. Meseck is a graphic and book designer in Germany, he graduated from the University of Applied Sciences Dusseldorf. Adrian currently lives and works in Dusseldorf.

p.144-145

Adrain Westaway
www.special-projects-studio.com

Adrian uses technology to make magic. His backgrounds in Electronic Engineering and Industrial Design combined with the fact that he is a full member of the Magic Circle helps him to understand how things work, and how they will work in the future while at the same time keeping a strong focus on interaction and experience. He is a tutor in Design & Innovation at Goldsmiths and Queen Mary University of London, and he is also a visiting faculty member at the Copenhagen Institute of Interaction Design.

p.020-021

Agata Bujko
www.behance.net/agata-9365ba

Agata Bujko came from Lithuania, and now she is a student of Academy of Fine Arts in Gdansk, Poland.

p.212-213

Agnė Dautartaitė –Krutulė
www.typography.lt

After the graduation of Vilnius Academy of Arts (VAA) Agnė Dautartaitė –Krutulė worked in the publishing houses, advertising agencies and designed interiors, but the love for books was getting stronger. So she decided to become a book designer and devoted her passion to book art. In 2013, her works won the prize of Experimental Book of the Year in the competition "The Most Beautiful Books in Lithuania".

p.114-115

Agnieszka Markowska-Jarzynska
www.agnesmj.co.uk

Agnieszka Markowska-Jarzynska is a Polish graphic designer specializing in design for publishing. Agnes worked for Housing Association "HUTNIK" in Zawiercie, Poland almost 14 years, till she moved to Dereham, UK. In 2004 she enjoys various aspects of design. Agnes enjoys experimenting with book design, and exploring her own images and illustrative elements. She is interested in interactivity and the animated effects introduced into design.

p.164-165

Ainorwei Lin
www.behance.net/Ainorwei_Lin

Ainorwei Lin is a 23 year-old designer based in Tainan, Taiwan. He is studying Digital Content & Applied Design at the STUST. And his works are ranging from print to conceptual projects.

p.136-137

Akira Kusaka
www.akira-kusaka-illustration.tumblr.com

Akira Kusaka is a freelance illustrator and graphic designer, now he is living in Osaka Japan. He creates for advertisements, book covers, children's picture book, web design, etc. He is not only an illustrator but also a trombone player in a two-man band called "Repair".

p.122-123

Alesia Yurtsevich (Iurtcevich)
www.behance.net/yur0a

Alesia Yurtsevich (Iurtcevich) was born in Kaliningrad, Russia in 1994. She is now a second-year student in graphic design major and earning her bachelor degree.

p.190-191

Alexandra Tuck
www.alexandraemilietuck.co.uk

Alexandra Tuck is a thoughtful and considerate designer, who's particularly fond of print and editorial design. She finds inspiration in everything, especially traditional crafts. Based in the North West UK, in the beautiful Lake District, she has a love for nature and being outdoors, as well as travelling and experiencing new cultures.

p.086-087

And Atelier
www.and-atelier.com

And Atelier is an independent design studio based in Porto, Portugal, which is founded by João Araújo and Rita Huet. They have been working mainly in the editorial area and poster design, and their works always try to accomplish a strong conceptual approach, through very clean solutions and with a strong typographic component and respect.

p.142-143

Arushi Khandelwal
www.behance.net/K_aaru

Arushi Khandelwal is a graphic design student from Banasthali University. Her main areas of interest are advertising, publication, typography, copy-writing and photography. She used to work as an intern in UNICEF and R K Swamy BBDO.

p.104-105

B

Bianca Luyt
www.behance.net/biancaluyt

Bianca Luyt is a creative designer from the streets of Cape Town, South Africa. She grew up with the love for all things beautiful in the buzzing city of Cape Town, which is filled with uniqueness and diverse people. To pursue her career in graphic design she moved to Germany in 2013 and now resides in Munich. She loves, learns, explores and appreciates all things about design. For her, there is nothing like a clean sheet of paper waiting to be used as a platform for creativity.

p.192-193

Biaugust
www. biaugust.com

Owen Chuang and Cloud Lu are two boys both born in August, they established "Biaugust" in Taipei in 2005. Their projects included graphic design, product design, space installation, and art creation, etc. Regarding "Life & Emotion" as the main idea of design, they hope the world could be changed into a better place by the power of design.

p.162-163 & p.166-167 & p.172-173

C

Calvin Tan
www.behance.net/calvintandou

Calvin Tan is a designer from Malaysia. Being multidisciplinary enabled Calvin to take on diverse range of projects including branding, packaging, digital art, editorial design, illustration, and mixed media. Besides, Calvin loves to show craftsmanship in his works and the attention of every single detail of them precisely and patiently, in order to show the passion through his projects and to the audiences.

p.148-149

Chanel Stracey
www.chanelstracey.co.ou

Chanel Stracey enjoys challenges and has interest in all areas of design, especially branding and packaging. She had developed strong interests in these fields when she was in university and would like to further develop her skills in the industry.

p.062-063

Chris Page
www.chris-page.co.uk

Chris Page is a multidisciplinary graphic designer based in London. His varied portfolio includes projects ranging from branding to print, packaging to restaurant and retail design. Since graduating Chris has had the chance to work in a number of award-winning design agencies.

p.224-225

Cristina Bianchi
www.cristinabianchi.it

Cristina Bianchi is an Italian graphic designer and art director who is now based in Vienna, Austria. She has worked in Italy and Austria for different agencies, and developed experience in graphic design and art direction, editorial and print design, packaging, branding and visual identity.

p.189 & p.210-211

D

Davide Ronco
www.behance.net/Wronco

Davide Ronco is an industrial design student at IUAV (Istituto Universitario di Architettura di Venezia). His passion derives from his family: his father, an architect and painter, and his mother, a ceramist and art lover, he grew up in a fertile ambient for creativity.

p.010-011

Dennis Koay
www.behance.net/dennis_koay

Dennis Koay is a graphic designer who thinks design is his driving passion. Dennis gets joy from the process of understanding how great design works, and he loves creating beautiful designs himself.

p.148-149

DESIGNCLUB
www.design-club.gr

DESIGNCLUB is a design studio based in Athens, Greece. It offers complete services of visual communication design (conventional and digital) for a diverse range of clients across several fields of expertise. DESIGNCLUB was established in 1980 and ever since enjoys a great reputation based on the quality, the style, and the design excellence of its projects.

p.182-183

Dina Fiala
www.behance.net/dinafiala

Dina Fiala is a graphic designer from Los Angeles, California. She attended the University of California, Los Angeles, in Psychology, and then moved to Providence, Rhode Island to study graphic design. She completed the Graphic Design Certificate at the Rhode Island School of Design in 2014 and currently works as a designer for various companies.

p.036-037

E

Emilia Emigo
www.behance.net/Emigo

Emilia Emigo is a designer who owns six years of professional career.

p.152-153

Enrico Salis
www.enricosalis.com

Just after his graduation in interior design in Politecnico di Milano in 2009, Italian designer Enrico Salis started his own business, and worked between design and art. In 2010, he established his own design studio in Brazil, actually in the city of Rio de Janeiro. His works are the results of visions and the researches of design innovative and functional solutions. His works included residential and commercial design projects in Brazil as well as in Italy.

p.094-095

Ermolaev Bureau
www.vladermolaev.com

Ermolaev Bureau specialized in visual brand creation, visual strategy development and project implementation in the sphere of corporate and consumer's communication and aesthetics.

p.208-209

Eszter Varga
www.Behance.net/esztervarga

Eszter Varga is a student of Budapest College of Communication, Business and Art in Hungary. She also loves package design, graphic design and web design.

p.040-041

Éva Somogyi
www.evagrafika.blogspot.com

Éva Somogyi is a graphic designer from Hungary, who owns a master degree of University of West Hungary, Institute of Applied Arts, Packaging and Graphic Design department, her professional areas are unique book design, book illustrations and pop-up books.

p.126-129

G

Gideon Dagan
www.DaganDesign.com

Gideon Dagan is an award winning industrial designer and inventor. He is best known for his innovative Perpetual Calendar and Time Sphere Clock designed for The Museum of Modern Art, New York. Dagan's work is noted for its contemporary, pure minimalist and functional design. Dagan has designed numerous industrial and consumer products including handheld computers, electronic instruments and furniture.

p.058-059

Gonçalo Campos
www.goncalocampos.com

Gonçalo Campos is a Portuguese designer who prides in finding surprising solutions, through the sound combination of materials and production methods, in a process that starts from within the object. He takes advantage of the available production methods leveraging their potential to develop ingenious and practical products. Known for a signature mix of humor and pragmatism, he collaborates with international brands, designing furniture, accessories, lighting, and consulting.

p.204-205

H

Hakan Aylan
www.behance.net/sihirlimantar

Hakan Aylan was born in Ankara, Turkey, who has been working as an art director in various advertising agencies since 2006. He is also giving retouching and CGI services for a company called Mr. Myope as a freelancer.

p.098-099

Hayon Shin
www.behance.net/hayonshin

Hayon Shin is a Korean-American and student at Rhode Island School of Design, class of 2016. She was born in California but brought up all around the world and has a vested interest in using visual communication as a mean to connect people across language, culture, and tradition barriers.

p.140-141

Hubert & Fischer
www.hubertfischer.com

Founded by Philipp Hubert and Sebastian Fischer, Hubert & Fischer is a design studio with offices in New York and Stuttgart, Germany with a global client base. The studio specializes in creating editorial design, type design, visual identity, print, application, websites and e-commerce design from concept to production. Hubert &Fischer has been recognized by publications and organizations promoting excellent designs, including D&AD, Page, the Art Directors Club New York, IdN, Gallery Mag, Computer Arts and Type Directors Club.

p.206-207

I

Iconick
www.iconick.nl

Iconick is a designer who loves creating ideas and working them out with a touch of creativity. He is driven to deliver strong concepts and quality designs while enjoys thinking in colors, fonts, elements and something visualized.

p.100-103

Ilona Neumaier
www.behance.net/ilona_neumaier

Ilona Neumaier is a German graphic designer specializing in typography and illustration. After her graduation she studied communication design for three years at the design school in Munich (Designschule München).

p.028-029

Isabelle Mattern
www.isabellemattern.com

Isabelle Mattern is graphic designer graduated from Luxembourg. She had built a design view that stands in between concept, perception, awareness, experimentation, interaction and experience expressed through visual communication, illustration and typography.

p.132-133

Ivana Vucic (Hamper Studio)
www.hamper.hr

Ivana Vucic is an award-winning graphic designer and photographer with particular interest in synergy of both media in a unique visual language. She was a co-founder of design studio Laboratorium (2001-2012) and today she runs Hamper Studio together with her partner Tom Jura Kacunic.

p.096-097 & p.186-187

Iwona Przybyla
www.iwonaprzybyla.com

Iwona Przybyła is a young graphic designer who was born and raised in Poland's magical Beskid Mountains. Despite having left home and living in the city of Poznan, where she lives and she did her master studies at the University of Arts, she feels bonded to her birthplace, which is apparent in many of her works. The main areas of her interest are typography as well as package and brand design.

p.202-203

J

Janilie Fleury
www.behance.net/janilie

Janilie Fleury is a multidisciplinary graphic designer, graduated from Université du Québec à Montréal (UQÀM) in 2012. In the past, she had worked for an agency specialized in publicity as an assistant art director and since almost a year, she is a freelancer in Montreal.

p.082-083

Jared Hansen
www.jaredhansendesign.com

As a designer, Jared Hansen strives to creatively think outside the box and beyond the now to generate purposeful and powerful design solutions. Jared also enjoys exploring the unknown and taking risks to produce something completely original.

p.018-019

Jekyll &Hyde
www.jeh.it

Jekyll &Hyde is an Italian graphic design and communication studio founded by Marco Molteni and Margherita Monguzzi in 1996. The studio's approach to design is based on close cooperation with clients, coordinated target-oriented planning and connection of all visual languages and media. Jekyll &Hyde design for Italian and multinational companies and institutions, ranging from technology to music and contemporary art.

p.016-017

Jennita Shah
www.behance.net/jennitashah

Jennita Shah is a student of ècole intuit lab, Mumbai. She is passionate about photography and design.

p.188

Jessie Ning
www.viggiero.com
www.jessiening.com

Jessie is an alumnus from Rhode Island School of Design. Besides being a committed graphic designer, she is also a serious classical pianist. Upon graduation, she founded Viggiero to create musical designs, as well as to further explore visual metaphors and transcriptions of music phenomenon.

p.214

Jodia Steenkamp
www.behance.net/jodiasteenkamp

Jodia Steenkamp studied at the well acclaimed Stellenbosch Academy of Design and Photography in South Africa where she received her BA in Applied Design, majoring in graphic design. Jodia's unmitigated passion for design is her attempt to figure out ways of redesigning, forging tangible research and communicating it where humans are encoded within the language component of her design processes.

p.054-057

Jodie-Ann Langley
www.cargocollective.com/jodieannlangley

Jodie-Ann Langley is a designer interested in most areas of design, particularly typography and print.

p.146-147

Julia Adelova
www.behance.net/4eharda_u

Julia Adelova is a graphic designer and illustrator from Moscow. She likes to invent something interesting in design, like drawing, photography and yoga.

p.196-197 & p.220-221 & p.232

Justyna Koc
www.Behance.net/justynakoc

Justyne Koc was born in Warsaw in 1987, she has been studying graphic design in Academy of Fine Arts in Warsaw since 2012, and currently in her IV year in this school.

p.184-185

K

Kara Collins
www.behance.net/karacollins

Kara Collins is a student in the graphic design major at Western Michigan University, and she has strong passion for design career.

p.180-181

Karina Ebner
www.behance.net/ebner_karina

Karina Ebner is a graphic designer who loves different ideas about design.

p.022-023

Kate Fawcett
www.behance.net/katefawce)design

Kate Fawcett is a graphic designer from the city of Bath, UK. With a passion for visual identities and a love for the tactile nature of publications and printed material, she was set on a career within the design industry from very early age.

p.090-091

Katsumi Tamura
www.goodmorning.co.jp/

Katsumi Tamura is the president of Good Morning Inc. His business activities included brand development and promotion, CI and VI, information design, sales promotion, website design, planning, production and sales of original products.

p.174-175

Kelan O Nuallain
www.behance.net/kbon

Kelan O Nuallain is an Irish graphic designer. He specializes in typography and photography and attended Visual Communication Design in the Institute of Art, Design and Technology (ADT) Dun Laoghaire.

p.160-161

Kolle Rebbe
www.kolle-rebbe.de

Kolle Rebber operates globally out of Hamburg. Employees from over 30 different nations develop cutting-edge creative for worldwide advertising campaigns.

p.044-045

Kostantia Manthou
www.Kostantiamanthou.com

Kostantia Manthou is an architect, a designer but mainly a craftsman. She is working among several disciplines exploring the new ways and meanings of handicraft. She has worked under the guidance of the Campana brothers for some years; since 2008 she has been working as a freelance designer and consultant, dealing mainly with product design and interior design. She has participated in various art and design fairs and exhibitions including Venice Biennial, Nuit Blanche, and Salone Del Mobile, etc. From 2010 she has been working as an assistant lecturer at Scuola Politecnica di Design. She currently lives and works in Milan carrying several obsessions regarding methods and materials.

p.108-109

Kristin Øverlie Edøy
www.kristinedoy.com

Kristin Øverlie Edøy is a Norwegian graphic designer from Australia, who loves all forms of creativity and design.

p.116-117

L

Laura Wallbridge-Bruce
www.behance.net/laurawallbridgebruce

Laura Wallbridge-Bruce is currently a third year graphic design student at Leeds College of Art. She has a passion for all areas of graphic design, packaging in particular.

p.120-121

Lee Jaegoo
www.behance.net/jack2

Lee Jaegoo is a designer from Republic of Korea, he is now a designer in Republic of Korea Navy Media.

p.106-107

Liat Meadows
www.behance.net/LiatMeadows

Lait Meadows was born in Israel, and he's now living in Germany. He studied communications design at the "Ifog Akademie" in Munich and emphasized on corporate design, typography and photography.

p.064-065

Lihi Bar-Or
www.lihibaror.com

Lihi Bar-Or is a web & graphic designer who focused on typography, branding, print, and interaction design. His works are inspired by geometric shapes, lettering and architecture.

p.215

Lili Thury
www.behance.net/lilithury

Lili Thury is a student of graphic design and intermedia at Hungarian University of Fine Art in Budapest. She is a designer who loves experiment with lots of technique, media and material.

p.168-171

Lo Siento
www.losiento.net

Lo Siento is a small studio that specially enjoys taking over the whole concept of the identity projects. Its main feature is an organic and physical approach to the solutions, resulting in a field where graphic and industrial design dialogue, always searching an alliance with the artisan processes.

p.134-135

Lucia Freire Coloma
www.behance.net/dry

Lucia Freire Coloma is a creative and a graphic designer with a focus on print design. She is specialized in identity and branding, but she also has experience in other fields such as packaging and advertising.

p.042-043

M

Magdalena Strączyńska
www.behance.net/straczynska

Magdalena Strączyńska is a freelancer graphic designer who focuses on graphic design -- packages, identification and poster, and fine arts – drawing, linocut and photography. She has participated in many exhibitions in Poland and abroad.

p.194-195

Maïté Chapelle
www.behance.net/myTmind

Maïté Chapelle is a designer who has spent her time and energy in her designer career, she's now a fresh graduated and ready to take an active part in professional life.

p.078-079

Margarita Kurtser
www.behance.net/Ritaku

Margarita Kurtser is a freelancer graphic designer from Moscow, and now she works on different kinds of projects: editorial, animation and illustration.

p.066-069

Maria Deligiorgi
www.behance.net/m_del

Maria Deligiorgi is a freelance graphic designer, currently located in Athens, Greece, but working for clients all over the world. She's being involved in all kinds of projects, commercial or experimental, in 2 or 3 dimensions, and is always up for creating a custom design for every situation.

p.218-219

Maria Musienko
www.behance.net/ggmariamus

Maria Musienko is a designer and illustrator. She worked as an illustrator in the children's cognitive edition "Grow with Khabarovsk." Later she worked as art director of fashion magazine "Fashion Collection", Knabarovsk Vladivostok. For a long time she also works as a freelance designer and collaborates with printing companies in Japan and Korea.

p.198-199

Markie Dossett
www.behance.net/MarkieDossett

Markie Dossett is a designer who was born in Ohio and raised in a small, rural town in northern Indiana. She's now a senior at Ball State University in Muncie Indiana earning a Bachelor of Fine Arts Degree in Visual Communications along with a minor in Graphic Arts Technology.

p.024-025

Marleen Annema
www.marleenannema.nl

Marleen Annema is a Dutch graphic designer. Marleen has been studying Graphic Design & Communication at the Minerva Art Academy in Groningen since September, 2013. In July 2013 she took her degree in graphic design at the CIBAP-College in Zwolle.

p.176-177

Mattea Stahl & Tamara Haake
www.tamara-haake.de
www.wuidl.de

Mattea Stahl and Tamara Haake are two young designers from Munich, Germany. During these studies they had the great opportunity to work together, benefit from each other and create some lovely projects.

p.118-119

Maude Leclerc-De Guire & Maxime Levesque
www.levesquemaxime.com

Both having graduated from the Université de Montréal in industrial design, Maude Leclerc-De Guire and Maxime Levesque tempt to use their skills to innovate in the conception of practical objects. Living and working in Montreal, their goal is to create sensible and accessible objects. They consider simplicity as the foundation of aesthetics, transcended by long-lasting design.

p.012-013

Muschi & Llicheni Design Network
www.muschielicheni.net

Muschi & Llicheni Design Network is a multidisciplinary network that makes communication actions in the visual art and design. This design agency designs identity systems for companies and cultural events, catalogues, editorial projects, web sites, video and interactive products. They think that design is really important for changing our life because it gives a concrete vision which is very useful for us.

p.178-179

N

Niels Kjeldsen
www.niels-kjeldsen.dk

Niels Kjeldsen was born in 1971, and he has been educated as an industrial designer. He started his own design agency "Niels Kjeldsen Design" in 2002. Since then he has received the Formland Prize as well as the Red Dot Award for his simple and elegant design. He has worked with companies such as B&O, Carlsberg, Stelton, Gubi, Nokia, Samsung and Loréal.

p.072-073

Nitzan Pode
www.behance.net/NITZANPODE

Nitzan Pode is third-year student in graphic design department of the HIT (Holon Institute of Technology) college in Israel, and she is a freelancer specializing in graphic design – Apps, Webs and Print.

p.014-015

O

Oksana Kapranova
www.behance.net/KshihaKapranova

Oksana Kapranova is a student of Kyiv State Institute of Applied Arts and Design. He is working hard to become the greatest graphic designer in his sphere.

p.075-077

P

Patrick Florville
www.florville.com

Formerly in pre-med, Patrick Florville is an award-winning creative director and brand strategist. Guided by a philosophy which goes beyond the typical aesthetics concerns, the success of his work is attributed to strong analytics – thoroughly understanding his clients' objectives and audience – and conceptual strength – bringing message and audience together through engaging and compelling creativity.

p.074

Pattapong Mekavarakul
www.pattapong.com

Pattapong Mekavarakul is a graphic designer who was born in Chonburi, Thailand. And he was graduated from Graphic Design Savannah College of Art and Design (SCAD).

p.088-089

Peter von Freyhold
www.vonfreyhold.com
www.typografie.de

Peter von Freyhold is a communication designer who is living and working in Hamburg, Germany. His awarded works are focused on editorial and corporate design.

p.158-159

Philip Stroomberg
www.stroomberg.net
www.thecubecalendar.com

Based in Amsterdam, The Netherlands, Philip Stroomberg is a graphic designer who works primarily in the cultural sector for clients including universities, publishers and art institutions. Stroomberg regularly creates designs that are used for the promotion of Dutch culture. Stroomberg is always looking to turn content into shape, and creating shapes based on content. An important feature of his work is interaction: his designs encourage the user to develop a bond with the object, and many of them challenge the users' imagination.

p.048-049

S

Sara Vrbinc
www.saravrbinc.com

Sara Vrbinc came from Ljubljana, where she completed her BFA degree in Visual Communication Design at Academy of Fine Arts and Design, and shaped her passion towards conceptual design. Currently she is on her Master's studies at Aalto University in Helsinki, researching creative processes that focus on hyper visual, contemporary graphic design, conceptuality and hybrid form of visual communication.

p.226-227

Sasha Tseng
www.Sashapure.com

Sasha Tseng is a designer always moving towards simplicity and refinement. Originally from Taiwan, Sasha came to America and quickly worked as an industrial designer. She first began at LUNAR and now she is working with HP. Sasha draws inspiration from the world around her, particularly the people she's encountered and the places she's visited. This wide-angle perspective makes her works more colorful, energetic and touching.

p.130-131

Sean Anthony Murphy
www.seananthonymurphy.co.uk

Sean Anthony Murphy is a graphic designer from London and he is interested in Print Design, Branding and Typography.

p.092-093

Sebastian Bergne
www.sebastianbergne.com

British industrial designer Sebastian Bergne is awarded for making everyday objects special with his essential and human approach to design. Sebastian's versatility allows him and his team to work in different ways. Sebastian Bergne works as an external industrial design facility to international brands, as a designer and supplier of bespoke objects for restaurants, retailers and individuals or even as producer of his growing collection of personal editions.

p.050-051 & p.084-085

Seoungkyeong Lee
www.behance.net/seungseung

Seoungkyeong Lee from South Korea is studying graphic design in London College of Communication. She loves graphic works and illustration.

p.070-071

Street Art
www.streetart.su

Street Art is a design studio based in Russia, and they believe in giving everything one's got to give and to share without reservations.

p.030-031

Stuart Greer
www.behance.net/StuartGreer

Stuart Greer is a visual communication student from Dublin, he is studying in the Institute of Art, Design & Technology (IADT), Dun Laoghaire, Ireland. His works include editorial design, spatial, identity, print, and web.

p.150-151

Studio Lin
www.studiolin.org

Studio Lin is the graphic design practice of Alex Lin. Their work process is founded on a desire to explore new territory through challenging collaborations with creative visionaries in the fields of architecture, industrial design, art and fashion. By combining the studio's analytical rigor with strong input from external forces, the resulting design is exponentially enhanced: 1 + 1 = 3. This formula also permits a fluid aesthetic to prevail.

p.138-139 & p.200-201 & p.228-229 & p.230-231

STUDIO NEWWORK
www.studionewwork.com
www.newworkmag.com

STUDIO NEWWORK is a graphic design studio based in New York focusing on branding, editorial, and fashion. They assemble a team of passionate typographic designers with commitment to search for excellence in design.

p.124-125

Sumit Vashisth
www.linkedin.com/pub/sumit-vashisth/52/68b/65

Sumit Vashisth is an art director with more than 10 years experience in editorial design, corporate identity and advertising in both Mumbai and Delhi, India. He has worked for a number of major brands and companies including FCB and Dentsu where he is currently working.

p.052-053

Susanna Hertrich
www.susannahertrich.com

Susanna Hertrich is a multidisciplinary artist working at intersection of design, art and technology. Her works include objects, sculpture, photography, video and devices. She illustrates moments of the strangely familiar by building unusual devices that seem to derive from a different normality. She has a number of publications to her name and her artworks are exhibited internationally.

p.009

Szani Mészáros
www.behance.net/szani_meszaros

Szani Mészáros is a student of Hungarian University of Arts.

p.038-039

T

Tan Say Fen
www.behance.net/fintan_belle

Tan Say Fen is a graphic designer based in Malaysia. Her desire of wanting to be distinctive among other starts her journey of art and design. She believes that art and design is an attitude of life as it leads her to observe the goodness of life. She loves rabbit, illustration and beautiful literature.

p.148-149

TBWA\ISTANBUL
www.tbwa.com.tr

TBWA\ISTANBUL creates many "disruptive" ideas for local and international brands it works with such as Akbank, Beko, Avea, Efes, IKEA, Aygaz, Ulker, Evyap, Teknosa and McDonald's. In 2013, TBWA\ISTANBUL was recognized by Advertising Age in Turkey as the "Agency of the Year" and according to Effectiveness Index, TBWA\ISTANBUL was chosen as "Europe's Most Effective and World's 9th Most Effective Advertising Agency". The agency was also awarded the title of "Agency of the Decade" by Capital magazine.

p.060-061

Tom Davall
www.tomdavall.co.uk

Tom Davall is a graphic designer based in Stafford, UK and recent graduate of Staffordshire University. He is a dedicated and conscientious person with a passion for design and typography, alongside having an interest in silk screen printing.

p.046-047

V

VASAVA
www.vasava.es

Since 1997 Vasava has taken the world by storm creating top notch design in an impressive wide scope of disciplines, ranging from custom typography, illustration, interactive design and animation. Vasava believes in passion, talent and technology in support of creativity, and continually find ways to push the boundaries of our crafted communication.

p.154-155

Vassiliki Kostoglou
www.kostoglouvassiliki.gr

Vassiliki Kostoglou worked as an exhibition designer at the Triennale Museum and popular design studios in Milano for 2 years, then she returned to Thessaloniki and has been working for the past 9 months as an architect while at the meantime designs projects of her own. She has participated in 8 exhibitions and in a number of contests, managing to receive the 3rd award in the "Greek Design, Good Design" contest.

p.110-111

Visitors
www.all-visitors.com

Visitors is a graphic design group base in Shanghai, China. It is founded by 2 visitors from Malaysia, Radio Woon and Howl Lee on December 2013. They intend to collaborate in all sorts of art and design projects across different creative industry.

p.112-113

Vladimir Masyuk & VOKAMA
www.vokama.ru
www.behance.net/vokama

VOKAMA is a design brand established by graphic designer Vladimir Masyuk. Under VOKAMA project Vladimir experiments with different materials and objects (graphic and object design).

p.080-081

Vladimir Repin
www.behance.net/reispreis

Graphic designer Vladimir Repin came from Russia, and his professional areas including: Graphic Design, Print Design, Brandings.

p.216-217

W

Walvis & Mosmans
www.walvismosmans.nl

Walvis & Mosmans is a strategy, communication and design agency based in The Hague, The Netherlands.

p.156-157

Winnie Tan
www.innietan.com

Winnie Tan was born in Singapore in 1975. She graduated from Temasek Polytechnic (Singapore) in 1995 and Kent Institute of Art and Design (UK) in 1997 where she studied Visual Communication. After 10 years of graphic/multimedia design and teaching experience in Singapore, she went to Prague (Czech Republic) to pursue an MA in Typeface Design at the Academy of Arts Architecture and Design Prague (VSUP).

p.222-223

Y

Yael Alkalay
www.behance.net/yael_alkalay

Yael Alkalay is an innovation strategy leader at IBM Mobile Innovation Lab. She's part of IBM's design leadership team, responsible for driving a culture of design and innovation throughout the company. Yael has over a decade of experience in developing and designing successful software applications and cross-platform products.

p.026-027

Yurko Gutsulyak
www.gstudio.com.ua

Yurko Gutsulyak is professional designer and art director with more than 12 years work experience. In 2005 with his sister Zoryana Gutsulyak he founded Graphic design studio by Yurko Gutsulyak (Kiev, Ukraine). Since the studio was established Yurko Gutsulyak was honored with more than 60 awards in design and advertising, including Red Dot, European Design Awards, Golden Drum, Communications Arts, HOW. He is the first in the history of Ukraine Epica Awards Gold winner.

p.032-035

ACKNOWLEDGEMENTS

We would like to express our gratitude to all of the designers and companies for their generous contribution of images, ideas, and concepts. We are also very grateful to many other people whose names do not appear in the credits but who made specific contributions and provided support. Without them, the successful completion of this book would not be possible. Special thanks to all of the contributors for sharing their innovation and creativity with all of our readers around the world. Our editorial team includes editor Laura Li and book designer Dongyan Wu, to whom we are truly grateful.